MW01678613

Red, White & Blueberries

From Classic to Contemporary, American Recipes to Celebrate!

Copyright © 2007 CQ Products
Waverly, IA 50677
All rights reserved.
No part of this book may be reproduced or transmitted in any form or by any means, electronic or mechanical, including photocopying, recording or by any information storage and retrieval system, without permission in writing from the publisher.

Printed in the United States of America
by G&R Publishing Co.

Distributed By:

CQ Products

507 Industrial Street
Waverly, IA 50677

ISBN-13: 978-1-56383-252-9
ISBN-10: 1-56383-252-6
Item #7018

Table of Contents

Introduction

O beautiful for spacious skies,
For amber waves of grain,
For purple mountain majesties
Above the fruited plain!

Those familiar words at the beginning of "America the Beautiful," written over a century ago, span the generations and still ring true today. America's rich harvests provide a bounty of food for tables across our country. *Red, White and Blueberries* embraces these foods and includes them in recipes that reflect classic to contemporary American cuisine. They are truly recipes to celebrate!

Anchors Away for...

Appetizers & Snacks

Warm Spinach-Garlic Spread

Makes 2 cups

1 (10 oz.) pkg. frozen chopped spinach
1 (8 oz.) plus 1 (3 oz.) pkg. cream cheese
¼ C. milk
1 T. olive oil
1 garlic clove, pressed or 2 to 3 tsp. prepared roasted garlic
½ tsp. salt
6 to 8 drops hot pepper sauce

In a medium saucepan, cook spinach according to package directions. Drain off water and press out extra liquid in a strainer. Cut cream cheese into small chunks. In a medium saucepan, combine milk, oil, garlic, salt and hot pepper sauce. Add cream cheese. Cook and stir over medium-low heat until cheese has melted and mixture is heated through. Stir in spinach. Serve warm with crackers or raw vegetables. Dip may also be chilled and served cold.

Thomas Jefferson hosted the first public Fourth of July reception at the Executive Mansion in 1801.

Reuben Dip

Makes 4 cups

- 1 (8 oz.) container sour cream
- 2 (8 oz.) pkgs. cream cheese, softened
- 1 (14 oz.) can sauerkraut
- 2 (6 oz.) pkgs. diced corned beef
- 6 oz. Swiss cheese, diced

In a medium bowl, mix sour cream and cream cheese. Drain sauerkraut thoroughly. Add sauerkraut, diced beef and Swiss cheese. Stir until well-blended. Spoon mixture into a small slow cooker and heat thoroughly. Serve with party rye bread or snack crackers.

Bacon Cheddar Cheese Spread

Makes 4 cups

1 (12 oz.) pkg. bacon
6 green onions, chopped
2 C. grated Cheddar cheese
½ C. chopped pecans
2 C. Miracle Whip

In a microwave or using a frying pan on the stove, cook bacon until crisp. Drain on paper towels and crumble bacon into small pieces. In a medium bowl, mix crumbled bacon, chopped onions, grated cheese, chopped pecans and Miracle Whip. Serve with snack crackers or toasted bread rounds.

Iowa, sometimes called the "Corn State," is a breadbasket for the U.S., with 90 percent of its land devoted to farming. The main products are corn and hogs.

Cheese and Chili Dip

Makes 3½ cups

2 T. butter, sliced
1 (16 oz.) box Velveeta processed cheese, sliced
1 (8 oz.) container sour cream
1 (10 oz.) can Ro-Tel diced tomatoes and chilies
1½ tsp. garlic powder
½ tsp. kosher salt

In a crock pot or nonstick 2-quart saucepan, combine butter, cheese, sour cream, tomato mixture, garlic powder and salt. Warm over low heat, stirring often, until melted and smooth. Serve with chips or raw vegetables. For a spicier dip, use Hot Ro-Tel or add hot pepper sauce.

What state is home for "cheeseheads?" Wisconsin, of course, also known as "America's Dairyland."

Everyone's Favorite Spinach Dip

Makes 3 cups

- 1 (10 oz.) pkg. frozen spinach, thawed
- 1 (1.4 oz.) pkg. Knorr dried vegetable soup mix
- 1 C. sour cream
- 1 C. mayonnaise
- 3 green onions, chopped
- 3 dashes hot pepper sauce
- Round loaf of sourdough or pumpernickel bread

Drain spinach in a strainer and press with paper towels to remove excess liquid. In a medium bowl, combine spinach, dried soup mix, sour cream, mayonnaise, chopped onions and hot sauce. Refrigerate for 1 to 2 hours to allow flavors to blend. Spoon the dip into a hollowed-out bread bowl or serving bowl. Serve with bread chunks, raw vegetables, crackers, tortilla chips, pita toasts or sun chips.

To prepare bread bowl: Cut off top third of bread loaf. Remove the bread inside and cut or tear it into chunks. Place bread bowl on a platter with bread chunks around it.

Party Shrimp Dip

Makes 1½ cups

1 (3 oz.) pkg. cream cheese, softened
1 T. mayonnaise
1 C. minced shrimp
¼ tsp. Worcestershire sauce
2 tsp. grated onion
2 tsp. chopped parsley
1½ tsp. lemon juice
¼ tsp. salt
3 drops hot pepper sauce

In a bowl, mix softened cream cheese with mayonnaise. Add minced shrimp, Worcestershire sauce, grated onion, chopped parsley, lemon juice, salt and pepper sauce. Blend thoroughly. Chill mixture for 1 hour to allow flavors to blend. Serve with crackers or potato chips.

For other delicious variations to this recipe, substitute minced crabmeat or lobster for the shrimp. Bleu cheese may also be substituted for the cream cheese.

Terrific Taco Dip

Makes 8 to 10 servings

1 (8 oz.) tub soft cream cheese

1 (15 oz.) can beanless chili

16 oz. grated Cheddar or Monterey Jack cheese

Preheat oven to 350°. In an oven-safe dish, spread the soft cream cheese. Layer the chili on top. Spread the grated cheese on top of chili layer. Bake until cheese melts and bubbles, approximately 8 minutes. Serve with nacho or corn chips.

Tasty Beer Cheese Spread

Makes 1½ cups

8 oz. shredded Cheddar cheese
8 oz. shredded Swiss cheese
½ tsp. minced garlic
1½ tsp. dry mustard
1 tsp. Worcestershire sauce
½ C. beer

In a medium mixing bowl or a food processor, combine cheeses, garlic, dry mustard and Worcestershire sauce. Slowly add the beer and mix until ingredients are well-blended. Refrigerate in an airtight container for 1 hour to allow flavors to blend. Serve with crackers. Store any leftovers in the refrigerator.

Pizza Sticks with Pizzazz

Makes 24 sticks

1 (10 oz.) can refrigerated pizza crust
1 T. melted butter
½ C. shredded provolone cheese
1 T. grated Romano cheese
1 tsp. dried basil
¼ tsp. garlic powder
⅛ tsp. cayenne pepper
Prepared pizza sauce, optional

Preheat oven to 425°. Lightly grease a large cookie sheet. Remove dough from can and unroll it on cookie sheet. Press dough into a 9 x 12″ rectangle. Brush dough with melted butter. In a small bowl, combine cheeses, basil, garlic powder and cayenne pepper. Sprinkle mixture over dough. With a pizza cutter, cut dough crosswise into 12 (1″) strips. Cut rectangle in half lengthwise to make 24 strips. Do not separate strips. Bake for 10 to 13 minutes or until golden brown. Remove from oven and re-cut along perforations. Serve plain or with pizza sauce.

Melt-in-Your-Mouth Mozzarella Sticks

Makes 6 to 8 servings

- ⅔ C. grated Parmesan cheese, divided
- ¾ C. dried Italian-style breadcrumbs
- ½ tsp. salt
- 1 (16 oz.) block mozzarella cheese
- 2 large eggs, beaten
- ¾ C. vegetable oil
- 2 C. prepared marinara sauce

Set aside 2 to 3 tablespoons of Parmesan cheese. In a medium bowl, combine the remaining Parmesan cheese, bread crumbs and salt. Stir well to blend. Cut the mozzarella cheese into 3½ x ½ x ½″ sticks. Dip the cheese sticks into the beaten eggs to coat completely. Allow excess egg to drip back into bowl. Coat cheese sticks with the breadcrumb mixture, patting to adhere and cover cheese. Place cheese sticks on waxed paper. After all cheese sticks have been coated, dip each one into egg and breadcrumb mixture a second time. Place breaded cheese sticks on a baking sheet. Cover and freeze for at least 2 hours. Breaded cheese sticks may be frozen up to 2 days before frying.

To fry mozzarella sticks, place oil in a large frying pan over medium heat. When oil is hot, place several cheese sticks into the oil and fry until golden brown, about 1 minute on each side. Drain fried cheese sticks on paper towels. Sprinkle with reserved Parmesan cheese and serve warm with marinara sauce.

Cheesy Fries with Dipping Sauce

Makes 8 servings

1 C. bottled ranch salad dressing (low-fat or regular)

½ (1.25 oz.) pkg. powdered taco seasoning

1 (32 oz.) pkg. frozen spicy French fries

4 strips bacon, cooked and crumbled

½ C. shredded Colby Jack cheese

In a small bowl, combine the ranch dressing and taco seasoning. Pour into small serving bowl and refrigerate until ready to serve. Place frozen French fries on a baking sheet and bake according to package instructions. Remove from oven and sprinkle shredded cheese and crumbled bacon evenly over the French fries on baking sheet. Return fries to hot oven until cheese has melted. Serve with the prepared dipping sauce.

Quick-Fix Franks

Makes 12 servings

1 C. ketchup
1 (8 oz.) can crushed pineapple with juice
½ C. grape jelly
1 to 2 T. chopped jalapeno peppers
1 lb. cocktail franks

In a medium saucepan over medium heat, combine ketchup, pineapple, grape jelly and jalapeno peppers. Cook and stir until jelly is melted. Stir in cocktail franks and heat through. Transfer to a small slow cooker for serving. Serve warm with toothpicks.

In the last 20 years of their marriage, President and Mrs. Washington dined alone only twice.

Classic Crab Cakes

Makes 8 appetizers

1 lb. crab meat
2 eggs
2 T. mayonnaise
1 T. finely chopped fresh parsley
¼ tsp. salt
Pepper to taste
Dash hot pepper sauce
½ to ¾ C. saltine cracker crumbs
Flour to dust cakes
2 T. extra-virgin olive oil
1 T. butter

In a large bowl, combine crab meat, eggs, mayonnaise, parsley, salt, pepper and hot sauce. Mix well. By hand, form 8 crab cakes, packing them lightly into shape. Roll each cake in the cracker crumbs and press crumbs gently into the cakes. Dust the cakes lightly with flour on both sides. Cover and refrigerate for at least 1 hour.

In a large skillet over medium-high heat, combine the olive oil and butter. Fry cakes 3 to 4 minutes per side until golden brown, turning once. Drain on paper towels.

Bruschetta

Makes about 12 servings

- 1 loaf of French bread
- 3 T. olive oil
- 6 Roma (plum) tomatoes, chopped
- 1 onion, minced
- 1 clove garlic, minced
- ½ tsp. dried basil
- ½ tsp. dried oregano
- ¼ tsp. salt
- Pinch of pepper
- 1 C. shredded mozzarella cheese

Heat the oven to 375°. Cut the loaf of French bread diagonally into ¾″ slices. Brush bread slices with olive oil. Arrange bread on a baking sheet and toast in the oven for 5 minutes or until golden brown. Reduce oven temperature to 250°. In a medium bowl, combine chopped tomatoes, minced onion, minced garlic, basil, oregano, salt and pepper. Stir well. Spoon equal amounts of the tomato mixture onto the toasted slices of bread. Top with equal amounts of shredded mozzarella cheese, pressing down lightly. Place the pan of bread back into the oven for about 2 minutes or until cheese has melted.

Bar-B-Q-Cups

Makes 10 servings

1 lb. lean ground beef
½ C. barbeque sauce
¼ C. finely chopped onion
1 T. brown sugar
1 (12 oz.) can refrigerated flaky biscuits
½ C. shredded cheese, any kind

Preheat oven to 400°. Grease 10 muffin cups. In a skillet, brown ground beef, then drain. To browned beef, add barbeque sauce, chopped onion and brown sugar. Cook over medium-low heat for 1 to 2 minutes. Separate dough into 10 biscuits. Place 1 biscuit in each greased muffin cup. Press dough against bottom and up sides to form a ¼ inch rim. Spoon ¼ cup of meat mixture into each biscuit-lined cup. Sprinkle each with shredded cheese. Bake for 10 to 12 minutes or until edges of biscuits are golden brown. Cool for 1 minute before removing from the pan.

Teriyaki Chicken Wings

Makes 24 wings

12 chicken wings
¼ C. light soy sauce
¼ C. dry white wine
2 T. sugar
½ tsp. freshly grated ginger
1 clove garlic, minced

Rinse chicken wings. Remove tips on wings and discard. Cut each wing in half at joint. Place wings in a large resealable plastic bag. In a small bowl, combine soy sauce, wine, sugar, grated ginger and minced garlic. Mix marinade well. Reserve 2 to 3 tablespoons of marinade for basting and refrigerate. Pour remaining marinade into the plastic bag, seal it and turn bag several times to coat wings thoroughly. Place bag into the refrigerator for up to 24 hours.

To prepare wings, drain off marinade and discard. Preheat oven to 375°. Spray a broiler pan with nonstick vegetable spray. Place chicken on the pan and bake for 45 to 60 minutes or until done. Brush wings with reserved marinade several times during bake time. Discard any remaining marinade after baking.

Spicy Buffalo Wings

Makes 20 wings

10 chicken wings
1 C. flour
1 tsp. salt
¼ tsp. pepper
½ tsp. paprika
½ tsp. garlic powder
½ tsp. cayenne pepper
1 stick butter or margarine
½ C. hot sauce
Vegetable or canola oil for deep-fat frying
Bottled ranch or bleu cheese salad dressing, optional

Rinse chicken wings. Remove tips on wings and discard. Cut each wing in half at joint. In a shallow dish, combine flour, salt, pepper, paprika, garlic powder and cayenne pepper. Coat the chicken pieces with flour mixture. Refrigerate coated wings for 1 hour. Coat the chicken pieces again with remaining flour mixture. In a medium saucepan, heat butter and hot sauce until butter melts. Reduce heat and keep mixture warm on stove top. Preheat the oil in a deep-fat fryer to 375°. Deep-fry the chicken pieces, a few at a time, for 13 minutes, turning once or twice. Drain chicken on a wire cooling rack for 30 seconds, then immediately put fried chicken into the warm buffalo sauce mixture on stove. Repeat with remaining chicken. Remove pieces with slotted spoon.

To make a spicier sauce, increase the ratio of hot sauce to butter. For a mild sauce, use ¾ cup butter and ¼ cup hot sauce. For a hot sauce, use ¼ cup butter and ¾ cup hot sauce.

Honey Barbequed Wings

Makes 20 wings

10 chicken wings
1 C. flour
1 tsp. salt
½ tsp. pepper
2 C. barbeque sauce
½ C. honey
Vegetable or canola oil for deep-fat frying

Rinse chicken wings. Remove tips on wings and discard. Cut each wing in half at joint. In a shallow dish, combine the flour, salt and pepper. Coat the chicken pieces in the flour mixture. Refrigerate for 1 hour. Coat the chicken pieces again with remaining flour mixture. In a medium saucepan, heat barbeque sauce and honey until warm. Reduce heat and keep mixture warm on stove top. Preheat oil in deep-fat fryer to 375°. Deep-fry the chicken pieces, a few at a time, for 13 minutes, turning once or twice. Drain chicken on paper towels or brown paper bags for 30 seconds. Immediately put fried chicken into the warm barbeque mixture. Repeat with remaining chicken pieces. Remove pieces with slotted spoon.

Tangy Meatballs

Makes 60 appetizers

1½ lbs. lean ground beef
¾ C. dry bread crumbs
1 egg, slightly beaten
¼ C. water
3 T. minced onion
1 clove garlic, minced
Salt and pepper to taste
1 T. vegetable oil
1 C. chili sauce
1 C. grape jelly

Preheat oven to 450°. In a large bowl, combine ground beef, bread crumbs, egg, water, minced onion, minced garlic, salt and pepper. Using a heaping teaspoonful, form mixture into 60 bite-sized meatballs. Brush a shallow baking pan with oil. Place meatballs in the prepared pan and bake for 15 minutes or until cooked through. Meanwhile, in a small saucepan, combine chili sauce and jelly. Heat until jelly is melted. Drain meatballs and place into a serving dish. Pour jelly mixture over the meatballs and serve warm.

Open-Faced Mini Reubens

Makes 24 appetizers

¼ C. Thousand Island dressing

24 slices snack rye or pumpernickel bread

½ lb. thinly sliced corned beef

1½ C. chopped sauerkraut, well-drained

4 oz. Swiss cheese, sliced

Preheat oven to 400°. Spread ½ teaspoon salad dressing on each slice of bread. Place slices on ungreased cookie sheet, dressing side up. Top each piece of bread with a slice of corned beef and about 1 tablespoon of sauerkraut. Cut cheese slices to fit bread. Place a slice of cheese over the sauerkraut on each piece of bread. Bake 10 minutes or until cheese is melted.

Blueberry Crunch Trail Mix

Makes about 5 cups

¼ C. melted butter or canola oil
3 T. honey
2 T. brown sugar
3 C. old-fashioned oats
½ C. wheat bran cereal
¼ C. raw hulled sunflower seeds
1 tsp. ground cinnamon
⅓ C. wheat germ
⅓ C. sliced almonds
½ tsp. vanilla extract
1 tsp. almond extract
¾ C. dried blueberries (4 oz.)

Optional ingredients: miniature marshmallows, peanuts, chocolate chips, dried apple bits, walnuts, white chocolate chunks, shredded coconut or macadamia nuts

Preheat oven to 350°. In a 9 x 13″ baking pan, stir together the butter, honey and brown sugar. Stir in oats, bran cereal, sunflower seeds and cinnamon. Bake for 15 minutes, stirring every 5 minutes. Remove from oven and stir in wheat germ, almonds, vanilla and almond extracts. Bake for 10 minutes or until golden brown. Remove from oven and immediately stir in dried blueberries. Allow mixture to cool thoroughly. Stir in additional ingredients as desired, before storing in an airtight container.

Glazed Nuts

Makes 2 Cups

2 C. almonds or other favorite nut
½ C. sugar
2 T. butter

Lightly coat a jelly roll pan or cookie sheet with non-stick vegetable spray. In a heavy skillet over medium-high heat, combine nuts, sugar and butter. Cook and stir for 6 to 8 minutes until sugar is caramelized. Spread the caramelized nut mixture on the baking sheet and allow it to cool. Break caramelized chunks into smaller pieces. The nut clusters may be stored in an airtight container for several weeks.

Banana Nut Trail Mix

Makes 6 Cups

2 C. oats

1 C. banana chips

1 C. roasted salted pumpkin seeds

1 C. peanuts or other favorite nut

1 C. raisins

½ C. butter, melted

Preheat oven to 350°. Mix oats, banana chips, pumpkin seeds, nuts and raisins in 9 x 13″ baking pan. Pour butter over mixture and toss until evenly coated. Bake uncovered, stirring occasionally, for 15 minutes. Cool and store in airtight containers until needed.

Salute to...

Soups & Sandwiches

Classic Chili with Cheddar

Makes 12 servings

1 lb. ground beef
½ C. chopped onion
½ C. chopped green bell pepper
2 T. minced garlic
2 small chopped chili peppers
1 (6 oz.) can tomato paste
2 tsp. chili powder
2 T. parsley flakes
1 (15 oz.) can kidney beans
2 (15 oz.) cans chili beans
1 C. shredded Cheddar cheese

In a large skillet over medium heat, brown beef. Drain off the grease and reserve to cook the vegetables. Set meat aside. In large pot, cook onion, pepper and garlic in reserved grease until tender. Add tomato paste, chili powder, parsley flakes, beans and browned beef to pot. Simmer over low heat for 2 to 3 hours. Stir in Cheddar cheese just before serving.

White Chili

Makes 24 servings

2 lbs. dried Northern beans
1 T. dried oregano
2 tsp. ground cumin
1½ tsp. seasoned salt
½ tsp. cayenne pepper
1½ C. diced onion
1 T. vegetable oil
4½ qts. chicken broth
2 cloves of garlic, minced
8 skinless, boneless chicken breast halves
1 (8 oz.) can of chopped green chiles

Preheat oven to 350°. Soak the beans in a pot of water overnight. Combine oregano, cumin, seasoned salt and cayenne pepper. Divide mixture in half and set aside. In a Dutch oven, sauté onions in oil until tender. Drain beans. Stir half of the seasoning mixture, beans, broth and garlic into Dutch oven. Bring to a boil, reduce heat and simmer for 2 hours. Cube chicken and coat with remaining seasoning mixture. Bake chicken on a cookie sheet in 350° oven for 15 minutes. Add chicken and chilies to Dutch oven and simmer for 1½ to 2 hours.

Broccoli Cheese Soup

Makes 6 servings

4 C. chicken broth
1 C. half-and-half
½ C. flour
½ tsp. dried minced onion
¼ tsp. pepper
4 C. broccoli florets
½ to 1 C. grated Cheddar cheese

In a large saucepan, whisk together chicken broth, 1 cup water, half-and-half, flour, onion and pepper. Bring to a boil over medium-high heat, stirring often, then reduce heat to low. Add broccoli and simmer for 15 to 20 minutes, until broccoli is tender but not soft. Stir in cheese and heat until melted completely. Remove from heat immediately.

Tomato Bisque

Makes 6 servings

¼ C. butter
1 small onion, minced
⅓ C. flour
2 C. whole milk
2⅔ C. tomato juice
1 (28 oz.) can chopped tomatoes
2 T. sugar
1 tsp. Worcestershire sauce
1 tsp. kosher salt
½ tsp. ground oregano
½ tsp. ground white pepper

In a large saucepan over medium-high heat, sauté minced onions in butter. Sift flour over onions, stirring constantly. Whisk in milk and simmer for about 10 minutes, or until thickened, and continue to stir constantly. Slowly stir in tomato juice, tomatoes, sugar, Worcestershire sauce, salt, oregano and white pepper and heat, simmering for 10 minutes. *Note:* to prevent curdling, heat tomato juice and tomatoes before adding to milk mixture. Serve promptly.

Thomas Jefferson grew the first tomatoes in America.

Black Bean Soup

Makes 8 servings

2 C. dried black beans, soaked 4 hours and drained

¼ C. olive oil

4 medium onions, coarsely chopped

1 T. minced garlic

2 carrots, coarsely chopped

4 celery stalks with some leaves, coarsely chopped

1 T. ground cumin

2 bay leaves

2 T. chopped fresh parsley

1 ham bone or ham hock

1 tsp. salt

1 tsp. freshly ground pepper

⅔ C. dry sherry

In a large kettle or Dutch oven, bring 8 cups of water to a boil and then add beans. Reduce heat to simmer and skim off any foam. Cover pan and simmer for 1 hour. In a skillet over medium heat, add onions and sauté for 4 minutes or until golden, stirring frequently. Stir in the garlic, carrots, celery and cumin. Sauté until the vegetables soften slightly, about 3 minutes. Add about ½ cup water from the beans. Reduce heat to low and cook for 20 minutes, stirring occasionally, watching to ensure that the vegetables stay moist. Add water as needed and remove from heat. Add bay leaves, parsley, ham bone, salt and pepper to beans. Stir in vegetables. Cover and cook for 2 hours, adding a little hot water if the beans become too thick. Remove the ham bone and cool. Once the ham bone has cooled, remove meat, put into soup mixture and discard the bone. In a food processor or blender, process the soup mixture until smooth. (This will need to be done in several batches.) Return to pot, add sherry and cook until hot. The soup may be garnished with parsley or lemon slices.

Scrumptious Beef Stew

Makes 6 servings

- 1 lb. boneless beef stew meat
- 2 small cloves of garlic, minced
- 1 T. cooking oil
- 1 (8 oz.) can tomato sauce
- 1 C. beef broth or 1 tsp. beef bouillon granules plus 1 C. boiling water
- 1 T. wine vinegar
- 1 tsp. sugar
- 1 tsp. salt
- ¼ tsp. ground cinnamon
- 1½ tsp. mixed pickling spices
- 2 medium onions, quartered
- 1 T. flour

Cut beef stew meat into 1″ pieces. In a Dutch oven over medium heat, brown meat and garlic in oil. Stir in the tomato sauce, beef broth, vinegar, sugar, salt and cinnamon. Tie the pickling spices in cheesecloth or put into a metal tea ball. Add spice container to the stew mixture. Bring mixture to boiling, then reduce heat and simmer, covered, for 1 hour. Remove spice container. Add onions to the stew mixture. Cover pan and simmer about 20 minutes more until onions are cooked and meat is fork tender. In a small bowl, blend ¼ cup cold water and flour. Stir into stew and simmer until thickened and bubbly.

Creamy Wild Rice and Chicken Soup

Makes 6 to 8 servings

- ½ C. butter
- 2 T. minced onion
- ½ C. flour
- 6 C. chicken broth
- 1 C. diced carrots
- ½ C. chopped celery
- 4 C. cooked wild rice (about 1 C. dry)
- 3 C. cooked, cubed chicken breast
- 2 C. half-and-half
- 1 C. milk
- ¼ tsp. salt
- ⅛ tsp. pepper
- 1 T. white wine vinegar

In a Dutch oven over medium heat, melt butter and sauté onions. Blend in flour and cook until light brown. Stir in broth, carrots and celery. Cook until vegetables are tender, approximately 20 minutes. Add the cooked wild rice, cubed chicken breast, half-and-half and milk. Mix in salt, pepper and white wine vinegar and simmer for 30 minutes, stirring frequently.

Holiday Potato Cheese Soup

Makes 4 to 6 servings

2 C. peeled potatoes, cubed
3 T. butter
1 small onion, chopped
3 T. flour
Salt and pepper to taste
3 C. milk
1 C. shredded Cheddar cheese
4 slices bacon, cooked crisp and crumbled

In a medium saucepan, cook potatoes in water until tender. Drain, reserving 1 cup of water. Set potatoes and water aside. In a large saucepan over medium heat, melt butter. Add onion and stir until tender, but not brown. Add flour, salt and pepper to onion and cook 4 minutes. Gradually add potatoes, reserved water and milk to onion mixture. Blend in cheese and bacon. Simmer on low heat for 30 minutes, stirring frequently.

Curried Shrimp Gumbo

Makes 6 to 8 servings

4 T. butter
1 C. finely chopped onion
1 tsp. minced garlic
2 tsp. curry powder
2 lbs. shrimp, peeled and deveined
2 (1 lb.) cans stewed tomatoes
1 tsp. salt
¾ tsp. crushed thyme leaves
Dash ground red pepper
2 T. lemon juice

In a Dutch oven over medium heat, melt butter. Add onion and garlic, and sauté, stirring until golden. Add curry powder and sauté 1 minute more. Mix in shrimp. With a sharp knife, cut through tomatoes in the can several times to break up pieces, then add tomatoes to the soup mixture. Add salt, crushed thyme, red pepper, and lemon juice. Bring soup to a boil, reduce heat and simmer, stirring occasionally until shrimp turn pink, approximately 8 minutes.

More than 150,000 oysters are eaten during the two-day St. Mary's Oyster Festival in Leonardtown, Maryland, each year.

All-American Cheeseburger

Makes 4 servings

2 T. mayonnaise
2 T. Thousand Island dressing
1 lb. lean ground beef
4 slices American cheese
4 hamburger buns, split and toasted
4 large lettuce leaves
1 large tomato, sliced
4 slices onion
12 dill pickle slices

Preheat grill. In a small bowl, mix together mayonnaise and salad dressing. Set aside. Shape meat into 4 patties. Grill patties over hot coals 3 to 4 minutes on each side or to desired doneness. Top each patty with a slice of cheese. Cover and continue grilling until cheese is melted, approximately 2 minutes. Spread 1 tablespoon reserved dressing mixture on each bun. Add cooked hamburger patties and top with lettuce, tomato, onion and pickles as desired. Serve immediately.

Egg Salad Sandwich

Makes 6 servings

6 hard cooked eggs, chopped
½ C. finely chopped celery
⅓ C. mayonnaise or salad dressing
1 T. chopped onion
¼ tsp. salt
Dash of pepper
12 slices of bread

In a medium bowl, mix chopped eggs, celery, mayonnaise, onion, salt and pepper. Spread about ⅓ cup egg mixture on half of the bread slices. Top with remaining bread slices.

The first Thanksgiving feast probably included cod, sea bass, wild fowl, deer, cornmeal, fruits and herbs. The meats would have been roasted or boiled in traditional English fashion. Breads were skillet breads cooked by the fire or perhaps baked in a clay oven.

Cheesy Tuna Melts

Makes 6 servings

6 slices French bread or other favorite
1 (6½ oz.) can tuna, drained
1 (3 oz.) pkg. cream cheese, softened
2 T. mayonnaise
2 tsp. lemon juice
1 C. shredded American cheese

Preheat oven to 350°. Toast bread lightly in toaster. Place on cookieshee. In a medium bowl, combine tuna, cream cheese, mayonnaise and lemon juice, stirring until well mixed. Divide mixture evenly on each slice of bread. Top with cheese and bake 10 minutes or until cheese is melted.

Easy Sloppy Joes

Makes 10 servings

2 lbs. ground beef
1 medium onion, chopped
½ C. ketchup
⅓ C. brown sugar
2 T. Worcestershire sauce
2 T. mustard
10 hamburger buns

In a heavy skillet, brown ground beef and onion. Drain grease. Add ketchup, brown sugar, Worcestershire sauce and mustard. Stir well. Simmer for 20 to 30 minutes, stirring occasionally. Serve on favorite hamburger buns.

Grilled Peanut Butter and Marshmallow Sandwich

Makes 4 servings

8 slices white bread
3 T. butter, softened
½ C. peanut butter
½ C. marshmallow crème

Heat frying pan to medium heat. Lightly butter one side of each slice of bread. Spread approximately 2 tablespoons of peanut butter on each of the 4 non-buttered sides of bread. Spread approximately 2 tablespoons of marshmallow crème on the other 4 non-buttered sides of bread. Place the marshmallow slices on top of the peanut butter slices, buttered sides out. Prepare like a grilled cheese sandwich, browning lightly on each side. Cut each sandwich in two and serve immediately.

Variations of this sandwich: Add sliced bananas, coconut or favorite jelly layer to peanut butter and marshmallow crème.

Grilled Veggie Sandwich

Makes 4 servings

¼ C. mayonnaise
3 cloves garlic, minced
1 T. lemon juice
2 T. olive oil
1 C. sliced red bell peppers
1 small zucchini, sliced
1 red onion, sliced
1 small yellow squash, sliced
4 slices of specialty bread of choice
½ C. crumbled feta cheese

In a medium bowl, mix the mayonnaise, minced garlic and lemon juice. Set aside in the refrigerator. Preheat grill for high heat. Brush vegetables with olive oil on each side. Brush grill tray with oil. Place bell peppers and zucchini in the middle of the tray and place onion and squash pieces around them. Cook for about 3 minutes, turn and cook for another 3 minutes. Remove tray from grill and set aside.

Spread mayonnaise mixture on one side of each bread slice and sprinkle each one with feta cheese. Place on the grill, cheese side up, and cover with lid for 2 to 3 minutes. This will warm the bread and slightly melt the cheese. Watch carefully so the bottoms don't burn. Remove from grill and layer the vegetables on the bread, serving as open-faced grilled sandwiches.

French Dip Sandwich

Makes 4 servings

1½ lbs. sirloin steak, sliced diagonally in very thin strips

Salt and pepper to taste

2 T. olive oil

3 T. butter, divided

¼ C. minced green onion

2 garlic cloves, minced

1 tsp. fresh thyme or ¼ tsp. ground thyme

½ C. dry white wine

1½ C. beef stock

4 French rolls

Season the beef with salt and pepper. In a large skillet over medium-high heat, heat olive oil. Cook beef in batches for approximately 2 minutes, or until browned on both sides. Transfer cooked beef to warm platter or baking dish.

In the large skillet over medium heat, melt 1 tablespoon of butter. Add onion, garlic and thyme and cook for 2 minutes, stirring often. Add the wine and cook until the mixture is reduced by half. Add the beef stock and simmer for 5 minutes. (This au jus mixture will be put into dipping bowls when served.)

Heat a frying pan to medium heat to toast French rolls. Use the remaining 2 tablespoons of butter and spread on insides of rolls. Toast rolls lightly in frying pan, remove immediately and set aside. Divide the meat and place in the four French rolls. Transfer the au jus mixture to dipping bowls and serve with the sandwiches.

Fillet of Fish Sandwich with Tartar Sauce

Makes 4 servings

4 small (4 oz.) firm, white-fleshed fish fillets

½ C. flour

Salt and pepper to taste

2 T. olive oil

2 T. butter

4 medium-sized crusty rolls, cut in half

⅓ C. tartar sauce

4 slices of cheese, optional

In a medium bowl, mix flour, salt and pepper. Coat both sides of the fish fillets with the flour mixture, brushing off excess. In a large skillet over medium-high heat, add oil and butter, heating until bubbly. Add the fish and fry until browned, about 3 minutes per side.

Generously spread each half of the rolls with the tartar sauce. Place the fish on bottom halves. If adding cheese slices, place on top of fish fillet before serving. Place tops on sandwiches and serve.

Fish lovers can go to the world's biggest fish fry in Paris, Tennessee, where visitors consume 12,500 pounds of catfish during six days of festivities.

Italian Meatball Sandwich

Makes 6 servings

1½ lbs. lean ground beef
½ C. grated Parmesan cheese
2 large eggs
¼ C. chopped fresh parsley
¼ C. crushed cornflakes
3 large garlic cloves, minced
2½ tsp. dried oregano
½ tsp. ground white pepper
½ tsp. salt
3 C. prepared marinara sauce
6 long French rolls, split lengthwise, toasted

Preheat oven to 350°. Spray a large, heavy baking sheet with nonstick vegetable oil spray. In large bowl, combine ground beef, grated Parmesan cheese, eggs, chopped parsley, crushed cornflakes, minced garlic, dried oregano, white pepper and salt. Blend thoroughly. Shape meat mixture into 1½″ balls and place on prepared sheet. Bake meatballs until just firm to touch and cooked through, about 20 minutes.

In a large, heavy saucepan, warm marinara sauce. Add meatballs to sauce and simmer until sauce thickens slightly, about 15 minutes.

Press center of roll bottoms to compact slightly. Spoon 5 or 6 meatballs into the depression of each roll. Spoon enough sauce over meatballs to coat. Place tops on sandwiches and serve.

Monte Cristo Sandwich

Makes 2 servings

Batter:

2 large eggs
½ C. milk
¼ tsp. ground cinnamon
¼ tsp. salt
½ C. flour
1 tsp. baking powder

Sandwiches:

6 slices white bread
4 (1 oz.) slices Swiss cheese
2 (1 oz.) slices deli ham
2 (1 oz.) slices deli turkey

Garnish:

Confectioners' sugar
Marmalade or jelly

In a deep bowl, whisk together the eggs, milk, cinnamon and salt. Add the flour and baking powder and mix until smooth. Chill while assembling the sandwiches.

To assemble the sandwich, layer (in order) a slice of bread, ham, cheese, bread, turkey, cheese, and another slice of bread. Secure sandwiches with toothpicks and cut sandwich diagonally into quarters.

Heat a sandwich grill (like a George Foreman) to medium-high and coat surface with butter. Dip the sandwiches on both sides in the batter and grill for 3 to 4 minutes, until golden and crispy.

Remove the toothpicks and dust with confectioners' sugar before serving with marmalade or jelly.

Grilled Ciabatta Chicken Sandwich

Makes 4 servings

4 single chicken breasts, flattened
1 (12 oz.) bottle Italian dressing
3 T. fresh rosemary
1 loaf Ciabatta bread
2 medium tomatoes, sliced medium thin
2 avocados, sliced medium thin
Freshly ground pepper
2 T. olive oil

Heat grill. Put Italian dressing and rosemary in casserole dish and add chicken. Marinate in refrigerate at least 30 minutes. Discard marinade. Grill chicken until cooked through. Just before the chicken is done, slice bread in rectangles, and then again horizontally. Brush each side of the bread with olive oil. Place bread on grill and brown lightly. To assemble the sandwich, layer in order, a piece of the Ciabatta, chicken, avocado, tomato, fresh ground pepper topped with another piece of Ciabatta.

Very few foods are invented. Most contemporary foods are adaptations of traditional food items. For example, today's grilled cheese sandwich is connected to ancient cooks who melted cheese on bread.

The Dagwood Sandwich

Makes 1 serving

The Dagwood Sandwich has its roots in American folklore because of the comic strip "Blondie," created by Murat Bernard "Chic" Young. According to the creator of the comic, the only thing that Dagwood could prepare in the kitchen was a mountainous pile of various leftovers precariously arranged between two slices of bread. Below is our version of the Dagwood.

- 2 slices multi-grain bread
- 2 tsp. mustard
- 1 tsp. horseradish sauce
- 2 lettuce leaves
- 6 pickle slices
- 1 slice of red onion
- 1 slice each of deli meats: turkey, beef, ham
- 1 slice each of deli cheese: Swiss, cheddar, provolone
- 2 T. sliced black olives
- 3 radishes, sliced
- 5 strips of green bell pepper

Spread bread slices with mustard and horseradish sauce. Layer the following ingredients: lettuce, pickles, onion, meats, cheese, olives, radishes and green bell pepper. Enjoy creating your own version of the Dagwood!

Star Spangled

Salads & Sides

Strawberry, Kiwi and Spinach Salad

Makes 8 servings

8 C. fresh spinach
8 strawberries
2 kiwis
2 T. raspberry vinegar
2½ T. raspberry jam
⅓ C. vegetable oil
½ C. chopped walnuts

Rinse and tear the spinach into bite-size pieces. Cut each strawberry into 4 pieces. Peel the kiwis and slice them. In a small bowl, whisk together the raspberry vinegar, jam and vegetable oil. In a salad bowl, combine the spinach, quartered strawberries, sliced kiwi and chopped walnuts. Toss with prepared raspberry dressing.

The California Strawberry Festival attracts more than 85,000 visitors to its annual event. It is the showpiece for the companies that harvest nearly 16 million trays of strawberries annually.

Cranberry Spinach Salad

Makes 8 servings

1 T. butter
¾ C. blanched and slivered almonds
1 lb. spinach
1 C. dried cranberries
2 T. toasted sesame seeds
1 T. poppy seeds
½ C. sugar
2 tsp. minced onion
¼ tsp. paprika
¼ C. white wine vinegar
¼ C. cider vinegar
½ C. vegetable oil

In a small skillet over medium heat, melt butter. Cook and stir almonds in butter until lightly toasted. Remove from heat and let cool.

Rinse and tear spinach into bite-size pieces. In a large bowl, combine spinach, toasted almonds and dried cranberries. In a medium bowl, prepare salad dressing by whisking together the toasted sesame seeds, poppy seeds, sugar, onion, paprika, white wine vinegar, cider vinegar and vegetable oil. Just before serving, toss spinach mixture with salad dressing.

Broccoli Salad

Makes 12 servings

1 bunch fresh broccoli
½ lb. bacon
½ C. chopped red onion
1 C. chopped celery
½ C. hulled sunflower seeds
½ C. raisins
¾ C. mayonnaise
¼ C. sugar
2 T. vinegar

Wash, drain and break broccoli into florets. In a heavy skillet or microwaveable dish, cook bacon until crisp. Drain bacon on paper towels and crumble into pieces. In a large bowl, combine broccoli, bacon, onion, celery, sunflower seeds and raisins. Set salad mixture aside. In a small bowl, combine mayonnaise, sugar and vinegar. Mix dressing well. Pour dressing over salad ingredients and stir to blend. Marinate salad in refrigerator for at least 30 minutes. Serve chilled and refrigerate any leftovers.

Tomato-Basil Salad

Makes 8 servings

Salad:

12 to 15 Roma tomatoes

1 small red onion

1 (2.25 oz.) can sliced black olives

⅓ C. crumbled feta cheese

Dressing:

½ C. vegetable oil

⅓ C. red wine vinegar

1 T. sugar

½ tsp. chopped fresh basil

¼ tsp. salt

¼ tsp. coarse ground pepper

Wash, peel and slice the tomatoes. Peel and cut the red onion into thin slices. Drain the black olives. In a large bowl, combine the tomatoes, onion, olives and cheese. Toss lightly and set aside.

In a small bowl, combine the oil, vinegar, sugar, basil, salt and pepper. Mix the dressing well. Pour dressing over salad, mix and refrigerate for 2 hours or more before serving. This salad keeps well in the refrigerator for 2 to 3 days.

More than 40,000 people come to the Pittston Tomato Festival in Pittston, Pennsylvania, to celebrate the tomato.

Tomatoes, Artichoke and Mozzarella Salad

Makes 8 servings

- 2 (14 oz.) jars marinated artichoke hearts, drained with liquid reserved
- 3 large ripe tomatoes, sliced
- 1 lb. mozzarella cheese, sliced
- 1 (8 oz.) jar roasted peppers, drained
- ¼ C. chopped black olives
- Fresh basil leaves

Drain and reserve the liquid from the jars of artichokes. In the center of a platter, place artichokes. Alternate slices of tomato and cheese around the artichokes. Scatter olives, roasted peppers and basil over the top. Drizzle with the reserved artichoke liquid. Let platter stand at room temperature for about 1 hour before serving to make the cheese more flavorful. This also makes a nice appetizer.

Picnic Potato and Egg Salad

Makes 10 to 12 servings

Salad:

3 lbs. potatoes, peeled and cooked just until tender

5 or 6 hard-cooked eggs

⅓ C. chopped red onion

⅓ C. chopped celery, optional

Thinly sliced tomatoes and cucumber for garnish

Dressing:

¾ C. mayonnaise

1 to 2 T. mustard

Salt and pepper to taste

Cool cooked potatoes, then cut into cubes. Peel and chop the cooled, cooked eggs into coarse pieces. Combine potatoes, eggs, onion and celery. In a small bowl, combine the mayonnaise, mustard, salt and pepper. Spoon dressing over salad and mix gently. If needed, add more mayonnaise or seasonings. Top with sliced tomatoes and cucumbers if desired.

Copper Penny Carrots

Makes 10 to 12 servings

- 2 lbs. carrots, peeled and sliced into "coins"
- 1 small green pepper, thinly sliced
- 1 medium onion, thinly sliced
- 1 (10 oz.) can condensed tomato soup
- ½ C. salad oil
- 1 C. sugar
- ¾ C. apple cider vinegar
- ½ tsp. dry mustard
- 1 tsp. Worcestershire sauce

Cook carrots in salted water until crisp-tender. Rinse well. In a medium serving bowl, arrange a layer of carrots, green pepper and onions. Set aside. In a medium saucepan, combine tomato soup, salad oil, sugar, vinegar, dry mustard and Worcestershire sauce. Bring to a boil, stirring until thoroughly blended. Pour marinade over the carrot mixture and refrigerate until flavor is absorbed. This salad keeps in the refrigerator for 7 days.

Zesty Chicken Salad

Makes 4 servings

½ C. mayonnaise
1 T. lemon juice
1 tsp. lemon zest
Salt and pepper to taste
¼ tsp. tarragon
2 C. cooked cut-up chicken breast
½ C. chopped celery
½ C. seedless green grapes, halved

In a large bowl, whisk together mayonnaise, lemon juice, lemon zest, salt, pepper and tarragon. Stir in chicken, celery and grapes. Refrigerate covered for 2 to 3 hours or overnight. Divide into 4 equal portions and serve on croissant or lettuce leaf.

Early American cookbooks rarely included menus.

Waldorf Salad

Makes 4 servings

2 tsp. olive oil
½ lb. cooked turkey, cubed
¾ tsp. curry powder
3 large crisp apples
Juice from a wedge of lemon
4 medium stalks celery, diced
1 C. chopped pecans
½ C. white raisins
¾ C. mayonnaise
⅛ tsp. ground nutmeg
⅛ tsp. ground white pepper
Salt to taste
1 small head lettuce, washed and dried
Fresh parsley sprigs
Pecan halves

Heat olive oil in a large skillet over medium-high heat. Add the turkey and sprinkle curry powder on top. Sear in the hot oil for 1 to 2 minutes. Set aside.

Core and dice the apples, leaving the skins on. Place apples in a large bowl and sprinkle with lemon juice. Fold in celery, chopped pecans and raisins. Spoon the mayonnaise over the apple mixture and sprinkle with nutmeg, pepper and salt, then mix gently. Add the seared turkey and toss lightly. Refrigerate salad mixture for 1 hour. Arrange lettuce on salad plates and spoon the salad mixture onto the lettuce. Garnish with parsley and pecan halves. Serve immediately.

Delicious Seafood Salad

Makes 8 servings

½ lb. imitation crab meat, shredded

1 C. cooked salad shrimp

1 C. diced celery

¼ C. sliced green onion

½ C. low-fat mayonnaise

1 T. lemon juice

3 hard-cooked eggs

Lettuce leaves or croissants, optional

In a medium bowl, combine the crab meat, shrimp, celery and onion. Stir in the mayonnaise and lemon juice. Peel and chop the hard-cooked eggs and fold them into the salad mixture. Refrigerate for at least 1 hour. Serve as a salad on a lettuce leaf or as a sandwich on split croissants.

Italian Spaghetti Salad

Makes 8 servings

- 1 lb. uncooked spaghetti
- 2 tomatoes, chopped
- 1 green bell pepper, chopped
- ½ onion, chopped
- 1 cucumber, peeled and chopped
- 8 oz. shredded Cheddar cheese
- 1 T. Italian seasoning
- 1 (16 oz.) bottle Italian salad dressing

In a large pan, cook spaghetti in boiling salted water until not quite tender. Rinse in cool water and drain. In a large bowl, place tomatoes, green pepper, onion and cucumber. Stir in the shredded cheese and Italian seasoning. Add cooled pasta and pour salad dressing on it. Toss well to coat. Chill for 2 to 3 hours before serving.

Grilled Vegetable Kabobs

Makes 8 servings

8 oz. fresh mushrooms, cleaned

2 zucchini

2 yellow squash

2 red bell peppers

2 green bell peppers

2 medium red onions

2 ears sweet corn

16 whole cherry tomatoes

8 oz. teriyaki sauce

Wash zucchini, squash and peppers. Cut the zucchini, squash and peppers into 2″ chunks. Peel and slice the red onions into wedges. Slice the corn into 2″ pieces. Cook corn in boiling water for about 10 minutes. Preheat grill. Pour teriyaki sauce into a large bowl and add vegetables. Stir enough to coat vegetables and then remove them. Thread vegetables on skewers and place on grill over medium-hot heat for 20 minutes or until tender. Baste occasionally with teriyaki sauce.

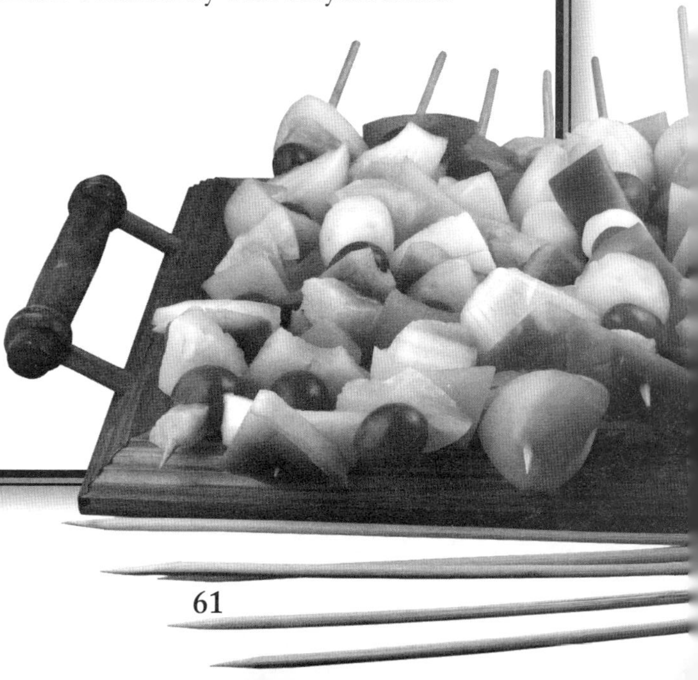

Oven-Baked Vegetables

Makes 6 servings

2 potatoes
1 carrot
2 onions
1 green bell pepper
⅓ C. fat-free or regular Italian dressing
⅛ tsp. garlic salt
¼ tsp. cayenne pepper
⅛ tsp. onion salt

Preheat oven to 350°. Peel potatoes, carrots and onions. Cut potatoes into cubes. Cut carrots and onions into slices. Chop the green pepper into small pieces. Grease a 9 x 13″ baking pan. In prepared pan, combine the potatoes, carrots, onions and green pepper. In a small bowl, stir together the Italian dressing, garlic salt, cayenne pepper and onion salt. Pour dressing mixture over vegetables. Cover and bake for 15 minutes. Uncover, stir and bake for 10 additional minutes.

Rum Raisin Squash

Makes 6 to 8 servings

1 large butternut squash
2 T. butter, divided
¼ C. raisins
2 T. dark brown sugar
Grated zest from 1 small orange
½ tsp. ground cinnamon
¼ tsp. ground nutmeg
¾ C. orange juice
2 T. dark rum
¾ C. broken pecan pieces, optional

Preheat oven to 325°. Cut the squash in half, hollowing out seeds and pulp. Use 1 teaspoon of the butter to grease a 9 x 13″ baking dish. Place squash in dish, cut side down. Add ½ cup warm water to baking dish and bake 45 minutes. Remove from oven when squash is tender. Let it cool.

In a small bowl, combine the raisins, brown sugar, orange zest, cinnamon and nutmeg, mixing well. In another small bowl, mix the orange juice and rum, then add to the brown sugar mixture.

Remove skin from the cooled squash and discard. Cut squash into cubes. Arrange squash cubes in a greased 9 x 13″ baking dish. Spoon brown sugar mixture over squash and dot with small slivers of remaining butter. Add pecan pieces, if desired. Bake for an additional 20 to 30 minutes.

Holiday Sweet Potato Puff

Makes 10 servings

3 C. mashed cooked sweet potatoes, chilled
½ C. sugar
½ C. butter, melted
2 eggs, beaten
⅓ C. milk
1 tsp. vanilla extract
½ C. brown sugar
2 T. butter, softened
¼ C. flour
½ C. chopped pecans, optional

Preheat oven to 350°. In a large mixing bowl, combine the mashed sweet potatoes, sugar, melted butter, eggs, milk and vanilla. Beat until smooth. Spoon mixture into a greased 2½ quart baking dish.

In a small bowl, mix the brown sugar, 2 tablespoons of softened butter, flour and pecans until crumbly. Sprinkle mixture over the sweet potato mixture and bake for 35 to 40 minutes or until golden brown. This may be prepared in advance and chilled or frozen until needed. Allow a slightly longer baking time when cooking chilled mixture.

Roasted Garlic Mashed Potatoes

Makes 8 servings

6 cloves garlic, peeled
¼ C. olive oil
7 Russet potatoes, peeled and cubed
½ C. milk
¼ C. grated Parmesan cheese
2 T. butter
½ tsp. salt
¼ tsp. pepper

Preheat oven to 350°. Place garlic cloves in a small baking dish. Drizzle with olive oil, cover and bake for 45 minutes or until golden brown. When cooled, mash garlic and set aside. In a large pot, boil potatoes in salted water until tender. Drain and transfer potatoes to a large mixing bowl. Add the mashed garlic, milk, Parmesan cheese and butter to the hot potatoes. Season with salt and pepper. Beat to desired consistency with an electric mixer, adding more milk if necessary.

Hash Brown Casserole

Makes 8 servings

1 (10¼ oz.) can condensed cream of chicken soup

8 oz. grated colby cheese

½ C. butter, melted

1 small onion, minced

1 tsp. salt

½ tsp. pepper

2 lb. bag frozen shredded hash browns

Preheat oven to 350°. Grease a 9 x 13″ baking dish. Set aside. In a large bowl, combine soup, cheese, melted butter, onion, salt and pepper. Gently fold in the potatoes. Pour into the prepared pan. Bake for 35 to 40 minutes or until heated through and top is brown.

Bacon Scallion Mashed Potatoes

Makes 4 to 6 servings

2 lbs. potatoes, peeled and cut into 1″ cubes

4 cloves garlic, peeled

5 strips bacon, cut into ½″ pieces

1 C. thinly sliced scallions

½ C. low-fat milk, warmed

½ C. low-fat sour cream

1 tsp. salt

¼ tsp. pepper

In a large pot, cover potatoes and garlic with lightly salted water and boil until potatoes are fork tender. In a heavy skillet, fry bacon until crisp. Drain on paper towels, then crumble. Pour out all but 1 teaspoon bacon grease from the pan. Add scallions to grease and sauté until soft but not brown. Add bacon. Drain potatoes and return to pot. Mash potatoes with milk, sour cream, salt and pepper. Stir in bacon and scallions. Reheat, if necessary, before serving.

Bean Medley

Makes 8 to 10 servings

- 1 (16 oz.) can pork and beans
- 1 (16 oz.) can red kidney beans
- 1 (16 oz.) can lima beans
- 1 medium onion, chopped
- 4 strips bacon, cut into small pieces
- 1 C. brown sugar
- 1 C. ketchup
- 2 T. mustard
- 2 T. vinegar

Preheat oven to 350°. Drain beans and set aside. In a heavy skillet, fry onion with bacon strips until lightly browned. Drain grease from bacon and crumble. In a large pan over medium-high heat, mix brown sugar, ketchup, mustard and vinegar. Allow mixture to boil for a few minutes, then add beans, bacon and onion and mix well. Place bean mixture in a large baking dish, cover and bake for 1 hour. Stir. If mixture is still juicy, remove lid and place back into oven until mixture thickens.

What are "bean-hole" beans and who invented them? Bean-hole beans were first cooked in a hole in the ground by the Penobscot Indians of Maine. The first thing you need to cook bean-hole beans is a shovel!

Broccoli Bake

Makes 6 to 8 servings

2 (10 oz.) pkgs. frozen chopped broccoli

½ C. chopped onion

1 T. butter

1 (10¾ oz.) can condensed cream of mushroom soup

½ tsp. dry mustard

½ tsp. salt

4 hard-cooked eggs, chopped

1½ C. shredded Cheddar cheese

1 (2.8 oz.) can French-fried onions

Preheat oven to 350°. In a large saucepan, cook broccoli according to package directions. Drain and set aside. In a skillet or saucepan, sauté onion in butter until tender. Stir in soup, mustard and salt. Heat until bubbly. In a 1½ quart greased casserole dish, arrange half of the broccoli. Top with half of the eggs, half of the cheese and half of the mushroom soup sauce. Repeat layers. Bake for 20 minutes. Sprinkle French-fried onions on top and bake for an additional 5 minutes.

George H.W. Bush detested broccoli and would not allow it to be served on Air Force One.

Old-Fashioned Scalloped Corn

Makes 8 to 10 servings

3 (15 oz.) cans creamed corn

2 eggs

1 C. crushed saltine crackers, divided

½ C. butter, melted and divided

½ tsp. paprika

¼ tsp. pepper

Preheat oven to 350°. Grease a 7 x 11″ casserole dish. In a medium mixing bowl, combine the creamed corn, eggs, ¼ cup of the melted butter and half of the cracker crumbs. Pour mixture into the prepared casserole dish.

In a small bowl, mix the remaining melted butter, cracker crumbs, paprika and pepper. Sprinkle crumb topping over the casserole. Bake for 30 to 40 minutes, until topping browns slightly and corn is bubbly around the edges.

The Olathe Sweet Corn Festival in Olathe, Colorado, serves free sweet corn to more than 20,000 festival participants each year.

Swiss Party Bread

Makes 10 to 12 servings

- 1 loaf French or Italian bread
- 2 (10 oz.) pkgs. Swiss cheese
- 3 (2½ oz.) cans sliced mushrooms, drained
- 2 sticks butter, melted
- 2 T. onion flakes
- 2 T. poppy seeds
- ½ tsp. Lawry's seasoned salt
- ½ tsp. lemon juice
- 1 T. dry mustard

Preheat oven to 350°. Slice bread lengthwise, then in 1″ slices crosswise (do not cut through the bottom). Cut the Swiss cheese slices in half. "Stuff" the bread by placing Swiss cheese and sliced mushrooms in all cut areas of bread. There should be enough cheese to put 2 half slices in each cut. In a small bowl, mix melted butter, onion flakes, poppy seeds, seasoned salt, lemon juice and dry mustard. Stir well and pour over bread. Wrap lightly with aluminum foil and place on baking sheet. Bake for 30 to 40 minutes. Remove from oven and cut through to bottom of loaf before serving.

Cheesy Garlic Bread

Makes 10 to 12 servings

1 C. shredded Parmesan or Asiago cheese

1 C. shredded Monterey Jack cheese

1 C. mayonnaise

½ C. butter, softened

2 cloves garlic, peeled and minced fine

1 loaf French bread, cut in half lengthwise

1 bunch green onions, root and green ends trimmed and chopped

Preheat oven to 350°. In a medium bowl, stir together cheeses, mayonnaise, butter and garlic until thoroughly mixed. Spread prepared mixture evenly over the cut side of each bread loaf half. Sprinkle onions evenly over cheese mixture. Place bread, spread side up, on a cookie sheet and bake for 7 minutes. Turn oven setting to "broil" and broil for 3 minutes. Slice bread into serving-size pieces and serve.

Cheddar Biscuits

Makes 8 servings

2 C. baking mix
⅔ C. milk
½ C. shredded mild Cheddar cheese
¼ C. butter, melted
¼ tsp. garlic powder

Preheat oven to 450°. In a medium bowl, combine baking mix, milk and Cheddar cheese, mixing thoroughly. Spoon about ⅓ cup of mixture for each biscuit onto lightly greased cookie sheet and bake for 8 to 10 minutes. In a small bowl, combine butter and garlic powder. Pour over hot biscuits when biscuits are removed from oven.

Spoon Bread

Makes 10 servings

4 C. milk
½ C. butter
1 C. cornmeal
4 eggs, lightly beaten
2 T. sugar
1 T. baking powder
¾ tsp. salt

Preheat oven to 350°. Grease a 9 x 13″ baking dish. In a large saucepan over medium-high heat, warm milk and butter. When the milk begins to steam, add the cornmeal and cook, stirring constantly until smooth, approximately 2 minutes. Remove from heat and let cool.

In a medium bowl, whisk together the eggs, sugar, baking powder and salt. Add the egg mixture to the cooled cornmeal mixture and mix well. Spoon the batter into the prepared baking dish and bake for 30 to 40 minutes, until golden brown. Serve hot with butter.

George Washington had breakfast around 7:00 a.m., often eating corn cakes topped with butter and honey.

Hats Off to...

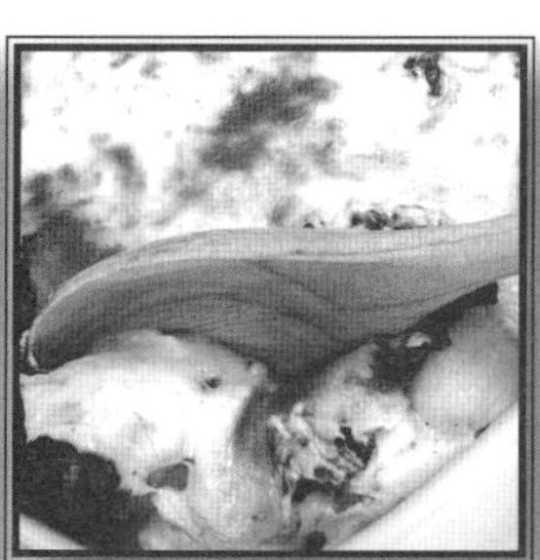

Hot Dishes

Classic Southern Fried Chicken

Makes 6 servings

3½ lbs. chicken, cut up
3 tsp. salt, divided
Vegetable oil
¼ C. butter
¾ C. flour
½ tsp. pepper

Rinse chicken pieces. Sprinkle pieces with 2 teaspoons salt. Place on a platter, cover with waxed paper and refrigerate 4 hours or overnight.

Pour 1″ oil into a large, deep, heavy skillet. Add butter and heat over medium-high heat to 375°. Meanwhile, rinse chicken under cold water. Place the flour, remaining 1 teaspoon salt and pepper in a paper bag. Shake well. Add half the chicken and shake to coat well. Shake off excess flour. Repeat with remaining chicken.

Preheat oven to 200°. Put chicken into hot oil in skillet in a single layer so pieces do not touch. (Cook the chicken in small batches.) Fry chicken until evenly golden brown on both sides, turning once after about 15 minutes. Drain well on paper towels. Place cooked pieces on an oven-safe platter in the warm oven until all have been fried. Serve hot.

Applesauce Pork Chops

Makes 4 to 6 servings

4 to 6 pork chops, ¼″ to ½″ thick
Vegetable or olive oil
1 C. applesauce
¼ tsp. brown sugar
¼ tsp. ground cinnamon
¼ tsp. ground cloves

Preheat oven to 350°. In a heavy skillet, sear both sides of pork chops in a small amount of oil. Place chops in a shallow greased baking dish. In a small bowl, mix the applesauce, brown sugar, cinnamon and cloves. Pour mixture over the pork chops. Bake for 1 hour or until tender.

Where can you go to eat the world's largest country ham AND kiss a pig? Go to the Trigg County Country Ham Festival in Trigg County, Kentucky, where tens of thousands of people go each year.

Classic Meatloaf

Makes 6 servings

1 T. vegetable or olive oil
½ C. chopped onion
½ C. chopped celery
½ C. chopped green bell pepper
1 C. ketchup
1 to 1½ lbs. lean ground beef
½ C. dry bread crumbs
1 egg, slightly beaten
½ tsp. salt
¼ tsp. pepper

Preheat oven to 350°. Place oil in small saucepan. Cook onion, celery and bell pepper in oil until crisp-tender. Stir in ketchup. In a large bowl, combine ½ cup of the ketchup mixture with the ground beef. Add the bread crumbs, egg, salt and pepper and mix well. Shape into a 4 x 8″ loaf in a shallow greased baking pan. Bake for 1 hour. Let loaf stand for 5 minutes before slicing. Pour remaining ketchup sauce, cold or heated, over meatloaf and serve.

Company Pot Roast

Makes 8 servings

3 lb. rump roast, fat trimmed off

2 T. olive oil

2 stalks celery, chopped

1 large onion, chopped

3 cloves garlic, minced

½ tsp. dried parsley

1½ tsp. dried thyme

2 C. beef broth

20 whole peppercorns

1 whole bay leaf

2 tsp. salt, divided

2 carrots, peeled and sliced

2 potatoes, peeled and cubed

⅓ C. flour

Preheat oven to 325°. In a Dutch oven, brown roast in oil. Remove meat from Dutch oven and set it on a platter. In Dutch oven, sauté celery, onion and garlic until tender. Add parsley and thyme and stir well. Return meat to Dutch oven. Add beef broth, peppercorns, bay leaf and 1½ teaspoons salt. Cover and bake for 4 hours, basting every half hour.

Add carrots, potatoes and ½ teaspoon salt. Bake for an additional 45 minutes. If desired, drain stock from Dutch oven into a medium saucepan and thicken with flour or cornstarch to make gravy. Slice the roast and serve on a platter with the carrots, potatoes and stock or gravy.

Marvelous Marinated Steak

Makes 2 to 4 servings

2 to 4 beef steaks, suitable for grilling

1 C. beer

1 T. brown sugar

1 tsp. Lawry's seasoned salt

½ tsp. pepper

¼ tsp. unflavored meat tenderizer

Place steaks in a shallow pan. Pour beer over the steaks and marinate for 1 hour in the refrigerator. Remove steaks from beer and discard beer. In a small bowl, combine brown sugar, seasoned salt, pepper and meat tenderizer. Rub mixture evenly over steaks and refrigerate for another 30 minutes. Grill steaks over a medium-high flame until desired doneness.

In the 17th century, meats were typically roasted on a spit and turned over a fire for hours at a time.

Saucy Baby Back Ribs

Makes 2 to 4 servings

- 3 lbs. pork baby back ribs
- 1 C. ketchup
- ¼ C. apple cider vinegar
- 3 T. dark brown sugar
- 3 T. Worcestershire sauce
- 1 tsp. liquid smoke
- ½ tsp. salt

Cut ribs into 2 to 4 serving sections. Place ribs in a large pot and add enough water to cover ribs. Bring water to a boil, reduce heat, cover and simmer for 1 hour or until ribs are fork tender. Meanwhile, in a medium saucepan, combine ketchup, vinegar, brown sugar, Worcestershire sauce, liquid smoke and salt. Bring mixture to a boil. Reduce heat and simmer uncovered, stirring often, for 30 minutes or until sauce is slightly thickened. Remove ribs from water and place them, meat side down, on a broiler pan. Brush ribs with half the sauce mixture and broil 4″ to 5″ from heat for 6 to 7 minutes. Turn ribs over and brush with remaining sauce. Broil an additional 6 to 7 minutes or until edges are slightly charred.

Tangy Slow-Cooked Florida Ribs

Makes 4 to 6 servings

3 lbs. beef or pork country-style ribs
Salt and pepper to taste
½ C. chopped onion
½ C. barbeque sauce
1 tsp. grated orange peel
1 tsp. grated lime peel
½ C. orange juice
1 T. fresh lime juice

Season ribs with salt and pepper as desired. Place ribs in a slow cooker. In a medium bowl, combine the onion, barbeque sauce, orange and lime peels, orange juice and lime juice. Pour over ribs and cook on low for 8 hours. Spoon sauce over ribs and serve.

Slow Cooker Sweet and Sour Pork

Makes 4 servings

2 lbs. cubed pork
1 (8 oz.) can pineapple tidbits, undrained
1 to 2 red and green bell peppers, cut into squares
3 T. brown sugar
½ tsp. ground ginger
¼ C. vinegar
3 T. soy sauce
2 T. cornstarch

In a slow cooker, place pork, pineapple, bell peppers, brown sugar, ginger, vinegar and soy sauce. Mix well. Cover and cook on low setting for 7 hours. About 10 minutes before serving, combine 3 tablespoons water and cornstarch. Stir into pork mixture in slow cooker. Cover and cook on high for another 5 minutes or until thickened. Serve over rice.

The Chitlin' Strut is held annually in Salley, South Carolina, and now attracts 40,000 to 60,000 people who eat more than 10,000 pounds of chitlins! Chitlins are boiled hog intestines.

Chicken Cordon Bleu in a Slow Cooker

Makes 6 servings

- 1 (10¾ oz.) can condensed cream of chicken soup
- 1 C. milk
- 6 skinless, boneless chicken breast halves
- 6 thin slices ham
- 6 slices Swiss cheese
- 1 (8 oz.) pkg. herbed dry bread stuffing mix
- ¼ C. butter, melted

In a small bowl, mix the condensed soup and milk. Pour a third of the mixture into a slow cooker, enough to cover the bottom. Layer chicken breasts over the sauce. Cover chicken with slices of ham, then slices of Swiss cheese. Pour the remaining soup mixture over the layers, stirring a little to distribute it evenly. Sprinkle the stuffing on top. Drizzle melted butter over stuffing. Cover and cook on low for 4 to 6 hours. This can also be cooked on high for 2 to 3 hours.

Balsamic Chicken

Makes 2 servings

1 tsp. olive oil
¾ C. chopped onion
4 garlic cloves, sliced
2 (4 oz.) skinless, boneless chicken breast halves
1 C. sliced bell pepper
½ C. balsamic vinegar
¼ C. sliced mushrooms
1 tsp. Italian seasoning
1 (14½ oz.) can diced tomatoes, undrained
1 C. hot cooked rice

In a large skillet, heat the oil. Add onions and garlic and sauté for 3 minutes. Add chicken. Cook chicken 4 minutes on each side or until browned. Add bell pepper, vinegar, mushrooms, Italian seasoning and tomatoes. Reduce heat to medium-low. Cook 20 minutes or until chicken is done. Serve over rice.

Our American Thanksgiving was declared a national holiday by Abraham Lincoln in 1863.

Island-Style Grilled Chicken

Makes 4 servings

4 skinless, boneless chicken breast halves
¾ C. picante sauce or chunky salsa
1 T. vegetable oil
1 T. lime juice
¼ tsp. garlic powder
½ tsp. ground cumin

Pound the chicken pieces to ½″ thickness using a meat mallet or a rolling pin. Cut chicken lengthwise into 1″ strips. In a medium bowl, mix picante sauce, oil, lime juice, garlic powder and cumin. Remove about ¼ cup of mixture and set this aside for basting. Add the chicken strips to remaining picante mixture and toss to coat well. Remove chicken from sauce and discard used sauce. Thread chicken strips, accordion-style, on 8 skewers. Grill 10 minutes or until done, turning and brushing often with reserved picante sauce mixture.

Chicken Stir-Fry

Makes 4 servings

4 skinless, boneless chicken breast halves
3 T. cornstarch
2 T. soy sauce
½ tsp. ground ginger
¼ tsp. garlic powder
3 T. cooking oil, divided
2 C. broccoli florets
1 C. sliced celery (½″ pieces)
1 C. thinly sliced carrots
1 small onion, cut into wedges
1 tsp. chicken bouillon granules

Cut chicken into ½″ strips. Place strips in a resealable plastic bag. Add cornstarch and toss to coat chicken. In a small bowl, combine soy sauce, ginger and garlic powder. Add mixture to the bag and shake well to coat chicken. Refrigerate 30 minutes.

In a large skillet or wok, heat 2 tablespoons of oil. Stir-fry the chicken until no longer pink, about 3 to 5 minutes. Remove and keep warm on a platter. Add remaining 1 tablespoon of oil to skillet. Stir-fry broccoli, celery, carrots and onion for 4 to 5 minutes or until crisp-tender. Add 1 cup of water and bouillon. Return chicken to pan. Cook and stir until thickened and bubbly.

Asparagus Swiss Quiche

Makes 6 servings

10 bacon strips, diced
½ C. chopped onion
1 lb. fresh asparagus, trimmed
1 C. shredded Swiss cheese
1 T. flour
¼ tsp. salt
⅛ tsp. pepper
1 (9″) unbaked pastry shell
3 eggs
½ C. half-and-half

Preheat oven to 400°. In a skillet, cook bacon over medium heat until crisp. Remove bacon pieces with a slotted spoon and drain on paper towels, reserving 1 tablespoon of the drippings in the pan. Sauté onions in the drippings until tender and lightly browned. Drain. Cut 8 asparagus pieces into 4″ spears for garnishing. Cut remaining asparagus into 1″ pieces. In a medium saucepan, cook all of the asparagus in a small amount of boiling water until crisp-tender. Drain. Set asparagus spears aside. In a large bowl, toss the bacon, onion, asparagus pieces, cheese, flour, salt and pepper. Pour mixture into the pastry shell. In a medium bowl, beat eggs with half-and-half and pour over bacon mixture. Top with asparagus spears. Bake for 30 to 35 minutes or until a knife inserted near the center comes out clean and crust is golden brown. Let stand for 10 minutes before cutting.

Fresh broccoli florets may be substituted for asparagus if desired.

Orange Pork Stir-Fry

Makes 4 servings

2 tsp. cornstarch
⅓ C. orange juice
⅓ C. teriyaki sauce
1 T. Dijon mustard
2 tsp. minced fresh gingerroot
1 tsp. minced garlic
½ tsp. grated orange peel
1 lb. pork tenderloin
1 T. canola oil
1 (16 oz.) bag frozen Japanese-style stir-fry vegetables
Hot cooked rice

In a small bowl, combine cornstarch and orange juice until smooth. Stir in the teriyaki sauce, mustard, ginger, garlic and orange peel. Set aside. Slice pork tenderloin into 2″ strips. In a large skillet or wok, stir-fry pork in the oil until no longer pink. Remove meat and keep warm. Add frozen vegetables to the pan. Cook and stir for 2 to 3 minutes or until tender. Stir orange juice mixture and add it to pan. Bring to a boil. Cook and stir for 1 minute or until mixture thickens. Stir in pork and serve with hot rice.

Hearty Green Bean and Sausage Casserole

Makes 8 servings

1 (16 oz.) pkg. pork sausage
2 (10¾ oz.) cans condensed cream of mushroom soup
1 C. milk
1 T. soy sauce
1 clove garlic, minced
⅛ tsp. pepper
2 (16 oz.) pkgs. frozen cut green beans
1 (2.8 oz.) can French-fried onions

In a large skillet, crumble pork sausage and cook over medium-high heat until evenly browned. Drain grease and set meat aside. Preheat oven to 350°. Lightly grease a 9 x 13″ baking dish. In a large bowl, combine the mushroom soup, milk, soy sauce, garlic and pepper. Stir well. Mix in the sausage and green beans, stirring well until evenly coated. Pour half of the mixture into the baking dish. Top with half of the fried onions. Spread remaining sausage mixture over the onions. Bake for 30 minutes. Remove from oven and sprinkle the rest of the fried onions on top. Return pan to oven and bake for 5 to 10 more minutes, or until the onions are toasted and the green beans are tender. Let rest 5 minutes before serving.

Egg Sausage Casserole

Makes 8 to 10 servings

1 pkg. refrigerated crescent rolls
1 lb. ground pork sausage
5 eggs
¼ C. milk
½ tsp. salt
1 C. frozen hash browns
1 C. shredded cheese, your choice

Preheat oven to 375°. Grease a 9 x 13″ baking dish. Press crescent rolls into prepared pan in a single layer. In a medium skillet, crumble and brown the sausage. Drain well. Spread cooked sausage over crescent roll crust. In a medium bowl, mix the eggs, milk and salt. Pour egg mixture over sausage. Sprinkle the hash browns on top of eggs. Sprinkle the shredded cheese over the hash browns. Bake for 30 minutes. This recipe may be doubled and baked in a jelly roll pan.

Grilled Individual Pizzas

Makes 6 servings

- 2 tsp. brown sugar
- 2 pkgs. active dry yeast
- 3½ C. unbleached white flour
- ¼ C. whole wheat flour
- ¼ C. cornmeal
- 1 tsp. salt
- 4 T. olive oil, divided
- ½ C. pizza sauce
- 8 oz. sliced mozzarella cheese (or cheese of choice)

Measure ½ cup very warm water into a bowl. Add sugar and yeast, then stir to dissolve. Let mixture stand 5 to 10 minutes or until a froth forms on top. Meanwhile, in a large bowl, stir together the white flour, wheat flour, cornmeal and salt. Make a hole in the middle and add 3 tablespoons of olive oil and 1 cup warm water. Add the yeast mixture. Stir together with a wooden spoon and then mix with your hands to form a ball of dough. Place dough on a floured board. Knead for 10 minutes until dough is smooth and elastic. Add more flour as needed if dough is sticky. Grease a large bowl with olive oil. Add dough, turning once to coat top with oil. Cover bowl with a towel and let dough rise in a warm place until it doubles in size, about 45 minutes.

While dough is rising, prepare desired sauces and toppings. Start a hot fire over a clean grill. Divide prepared dough into 6 equal portions. On floured surface, roll out dough to desired shape, about ½″ thick. Coat both sides of crust with olive oil, then place on the grill directly over the fire. Grill for about 2 minutes or until upper surface of dough begins to bubble. Watch closely and rotate with spatula if needed. When golden brown on bottom, turn crusts over and remove from heat.

Warm up pizza sauce in a microwave oven. Brush grilled side of crusts with olive oil and spread warmed sauce, cheese and pizza toppings on each crust. Pat toppings down lightly. Sprinkle some olive oil over each pizza. Return to the grill for 2 to 4 more minutes.

Baked Chicken Chimichangas

Makes 8 servings

1 small onion, chopped
3 cloves garlic, minced
1 T. vegetable oil
2 C. salsa
1½ tsp. chili powder
½ tsp. ground cumin
½ tsp. ground cinnamon
Pinch salt
2½ C. cooked, shredded chicken or turkey
8 (12″) flour tortillas
1 C. canned refried beans
Sour cream, optional
Guacamole, optional

In a large saucepan over medium-high heat, sauté onion and garlic in oil until tender. Stir in salsa, chili powder, cumin, cinnamon and salt. Fold in the shredded chicken or turkey. Remove from heat and set aside.

Preheat oven to 450°. Spoon 2 tablespoons of refried beans down the center of each tortilla. Place a scant ½ cup of the chicken mixture on top of beans. Fold the top and bottom of the tortillas toward the center and roll up the sides. Secure with wooden toothpicks or pieces of spaghetti noodles. Grease a 9 x 13″ baking dish. Place chimichangas in the prepared pan, seam side down. Spray chimichangas with a light coating of nonstick vegetable spray. Bake for 10 minutes and then turn them over. Bake for an additional 10 to 15 minutes or until golden brown and crisp. Serve with sour cream and guacamole.

Anytime Egg and Cheese Burritos

Makes 6 servings

- ¾ C. sour cream
- 2 T. taco seasoning mix
- 6 eggs
- 6 (8″) flour tortillas, warmed
- ¾ C. shredded Cheddar cheese
- 1 C. shredded lettuce
- 1 C. chopped tomato

In a small bowl, combine the sour cream and taco seasoning. Mix well and set aside. In a medium bowl, beat together eggs and 2 tablespoons of water. Spray a 10″ skillet with nonstick vegetable spray and heat on medium-low. Pour eggs into prepared skillet, stirring occasionally, until eggs are set, about 3 to 5 minutes.

To assemble burritos, spread 2 tablespoons of sour cream mixture over each warm tortilla. Top with a sixth of the cooked eggs and about 2 tablespoons each of the shredded cheese, lettuce and chopped tomato. Roll up tightly and serve warm. If desired, top with salsa, sour cream and cheese.

Baked Ravioli

Makes 6 to 8 servings

1 lb. ground beef, turkey or Italian sausage

1 (28 oz.) jar spaghetti sauce

1 (13 oz.) bag frozen cheese ravioli

2 C. shredded mozzarella cheese

In a skillet over medium-high heat, brown ground meat, breaking it up as it cooks. Drain well. Stir spaghetti sauce into the cooked meat. Preheat oven to 350°. Spread ⅓ of the sauce mixture over the bottom of a greased 9 x 13″ baking pan. Layer half of the ravioli evenly on top of sauce. Spread another third of the sauce over the ravioli. Sprinkle 1 cup of mozzarella cheese on top of ravioli. Make a second layer of ravioli, sauce and cheese. Bake for 30 minutes. Let pan rest for 5 minutes before serving with a large spoon.

Classic Lasagna

Makes 12 servings

½ lb. ground Italian sausage
½ lb. lean ground beef
1 small onion, chopped
2 cloves garlic, minced
1 C. red table wine
1 (14½ oz.) can stewed tomatoes
1 (15 oz.) can tomato sauce
1 tsp. dried basil
1 tsp. dried oregano
½ tsp. fennel seeds
Salt and pepper to taste
8 oz. uncooked lasagna noodles
2 T. olive oil
2 C. ricotta cheese
1 egg
5 T. chopped fresh parsley, divided
½ C. grated Parmesan cheese
2 C. shredded mozzarella cheese

In a large skillet, brown the ground sausage and ground beef with the onion and garlic, stirring until crumbly. Drain. Add the wine, tomatoes, tomato sauce, basil, oregano, fennel seeds, salt and pepper and mix well. Simmer uncovered for 2 to 3 hours.

Cook the noodles according to package instructions, adding the olive oil to the boiling water. Drain noodles. Meanwhile, in a medium bowl, mix the ricotta cheese, egg, chopped parsley and Parmesan cheese. Set aside.

Preheat oven to 350°. Spread a small amount of the sauce over the bottom of a 9 x 13″ baking dish. Layer half of the noodles, ricotta cheese mixture, and mozzarella cheese in the prepared dish. Spread on half of the remaining sauce. Repeat with a second layer, using the remaining ingredients. Sprinkle with remaining 2 tablespoons parsley. Bake uncovered for 1 hour. Remove from oven and let baked lasagna stand 10 minutes before cutting.

Taco Casserole

Makes 6 to 8 servings

1½ lbs. lean ground beef
1 small onion, chopped
1 (15 oz.) can tomato sauce
1 (1¼ oz.) pkg. taco seasoning
2 (15 oz.) cans refried beans
1 (13½ oz.) pkg. taco-flavored or plain tortilla chips
2 C. shredded Cheddar cheese
½ C. sliced black olives

Preheat oven to 250°. In a large skillet, brown the ground beef and chopped onion. Drain. Add the tomato sauce and taco seasoning. Stir well and simmer for 3 to 4 minutes. In a microwaveable dish, heat the refried beans for 1 to 2 minutes to soften. Break up the chips into smaller pieces. In a 9 x 13″ pan, spread a layer of chips. Dab on the softened beans. Cover chips and beans with meat mixture. Top with shredded cheese. Put sliced olives on top. Bake for 45 minutes or until cheese melts and casserole is heated through. Serve with salsa.

Baked Ziti Casserole

Makes 6 servings

8 oz. ziti pasta

1 lb. ground Italian sausage

1 (26 oz.) jar spaghetti sauce

2 C. shredded mozzarella cheese, divided

Preheat oven to 350°. Cook and drain pasta according to package instructions. In a skillet over medium-high heat, brown ground sausage, breaking it up as it cooks. Drain well. In a large bowl, combine the cooked pasta, sausage, spaghetti sauce and 1 cup of cheese. Mix well. Spread mixture in a greased 2½ quart baking dish. Cover and bake for 35 minutes or until hot and bubbly. Uncover and top with remaining cheese. Bake until cheese melts.

Drum Roll for...

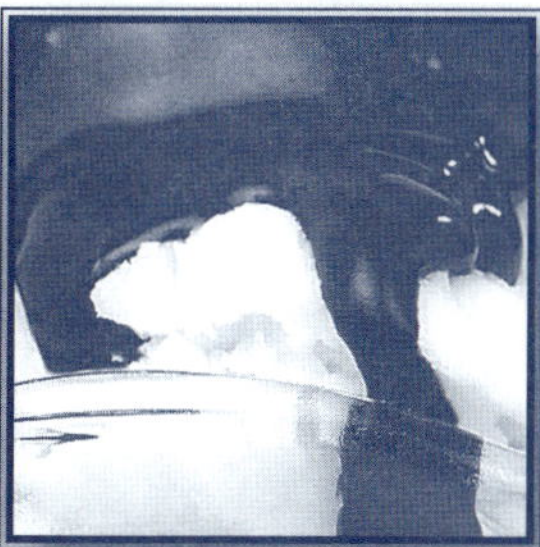

Desserts

Thumbprint Cookies

Makes 3 dozen

½ C. butter or margarine, softened
¼ C. brown sugar
1 egg yolk
1 tsp. vanilla extract
1 C. flour
1 egg white, slightly beaten
1 C. chopped walnuts
¼ C. currant or grape jelly or chocolate kisses

Preheat oven to 375°. In a medium mixing bowl, use a large spoon to beat the butter, brown sugar, egg yolk and vanilla until smooth. Stir in flour until well mixed. Refrigerate dough for 30 minutes. Roll dough into 1″ balls. Dip balls into beaten egg white, roll in chopped walnuts and place 2″ apart on a cookie sheet. Press thumb about halfway through the center of each dough ball. Spoon a small amount of jelly into each hole or press a chocolate kiss in place. Bake for 10 to 12 minutes.

Ronald Reagan loved jellybeans and always had a jar on his desk in the Oval Office.

Ginger Snaps

Makes 2 dozen

¾ C. butter or margarine, softened
1 C. brown sugar
1 egg
¼ C. molasses
2½ C. flour
1 tsp. ground cinnamon
1 tsp. ground ginger
1 tsp. baking powder
1 tsp. salt
½ tsp. ground cloves

Preheat oven to 350°. In a medium mixing bowl with an electric mixer, combine butter, brown sugar, egg and molasses until creamy. Set aside. In another bowl, combine flour, cinnamon, ginger, baking powder, salt and cloves. Add the flour mixture to the creamed mixture and beat until well-blended. Refrigerate dough for 1 hour. Divide dough into 2 portions. On a well-floured surface, roll out 1 portion of dough to ¼″ thickness. Use cookie cutters to cut 2 to 3″ circles or other shapes. Repeat with second portion of dough. Bake on a greased cookie sheet for 6 to 8 minutes.

Ice cream lovers can thank a vendor at the St. Louis World's Fair in 1904 for ice cream cones. Children at the fair were the first in the world to eat the delicious treat.

Soft Peanut Butter Cookies

Makes about 2 dozen

1½ C. flour
2 tsp. baking soda
½ tsp. salt
1 C. brown sugar
¼ C. sugar
½ C. butter-flavored shortening
½ C. chunky peanut butter
1 egg
1 tsp. vanilla extract
½ C. chopped peanuts, optional
Sugar for dipping

Preheat oven to 375°. In a medium bowl, combine flour, baking soda and salt. Set aside. With an electric mixer, cream together brown sugar, sugar and shortening. Beat in peanut butter. Add the egg and vanilla, then beat until well-blended. Slowly beat in the dry ingredients. Fold in chopped peanuts if desired. Place a small amount of sugar into a bowl. Roll dough into walnut-sized balls and dip one side into the sugar. Place on an ungreased cookie sheet, 2″ apart. With fork, press tops down slightly in a criss-cross pattern. Bake for 12 to 16 minutes. Allow cookies to cool on the pan for 1 minute, then remove them and cool completely on a wire rack. Store in an airtight container.

Jimmy Carter was a peanut farmer in Georgia before he was elected President.

Double Chocolate Cookies

Makes 5 dozen

2 C. flour
¾ C. unsweetened cocoa powder
1 tsp. baking soda
½ tsp. salt
1½ C. sugar
1¼ C. unsalted butter, softened
1 tsp. vanilla extract
2 eggs
1 C. semi-sweet chocolate chips

Preheat oven to 350°. In a medium bowl, combine flour, cocoa, baking soda and salt. Set aside. With an electric mixer, cream together the sugar, butter and vanilla. Beat in eggs until well blended. Slowly beat in the dry ingredients. With a large spoon, fold in the chocolate chips. Drop dough by teaspoonfuls on ungreased cookie sheets. Bake for 8 to 10 minutes. Cool for 2 minutes, then transfer cookies to a wire rack to cool completely.

Blueberry Bars

Makes 24 bars

1½ C. flour
¾ C. butter, softened
½ C. powdered sugar
3 eggs
1½ C. sugar
¾ tsp. baking powder
½ tsp. salt
¾ tsp. ground cinnamon
1½ tsp. vanilla extract
1½ tsp. lemon juice
6 T. flour
1½ C. fresh blueberries

Preheat oven to 350°. In a medium bowl, mix the flour, butter and powdered sugar, until well blended. Press into a 9 x 13″ baking pan. Bake for 8 to 10 minutes or until golden brown. In another medium bowl, thoroughly mix the eggs, sugar, baking powder, salt, cinnamon, vanilla, lemon juice and flour. Gently fold in fresh blueberries to this mixture. Spread mixture on baked crust. Bake for an additional 30 minutes. Cool completely before cutting into bars.

Fudge-Filled M&M Bars

Makes about 4 dozen

2 C. quick oats, uncooked
1½ C. flour
1 C. chopped nuts
1 C. brown sugar
1 tsp. baking soda
¾ tsp. salt
1 C. margarine, melted
2 T. margarine
1½ C. plain M & M chocolate candies, divided
1 (14 oz.) can sweetened condensed milk

Preheat oven to 375°. Grease a 10½ x 15½″ jelly roll pan. In a large bowl, mix oats, flour, chopped nuts, brown sugar, baking soda and salt. Stir in 1 cup melted margarine until mixture resembles coarse crumbs. Reserve 1½ cups of the crumbly mixture. Press remaining crumbly mixture into prepared pan. Bake for 10 minutes. In a small saucepan, heat 2 tablespoons margarine until melted. Stir in 1 cup of the candies. Press candies with the back of a spoon until they break into pieces. Cook and stir until chocolate melts. Pieces of candy coating will remain. Remove from heat. Stir in sweetened condensed milk. Spread chocolate mixture over baked layer to within ½″ of edges. Mix reserved crumbly mixture with remaining candies. Sprinkle evenly over chocolate mixture. Press down lightly. Bake for 20 minutes or until golden brown. Cool and cut into bars.

S'Mores Bars

Makes 24 bars

2 C. graham cracker crumbs
⅓ C. sugar
¼ tsp. salt
½ C. unsalted butter, melted
1 lb. milk chocolate
4 C. miniature marshmallows

Preheat oven to 350°. In a medium bowl, combine the crumbs, sugar, salt and melted butter. Mix well. Reserve 1 cup of the mixture and set aside. Press the remaining mixture into the bottom of a greased 9 x 13″ baking dish. Bake the crust for 12 minutes or until golden brown. Let pan cool on a rack. In a microwave-safe bowl, break chocolate into pieces and cook in microwave on high for 30-second intervals until chocolate is melted. Pour melted chocolate over the baked crust and spread it evenly. Sprinkle marshmallows on top of chocolate, pressing them lightly. Sprinkle reserved crumb mixture over marshmallows. Broil the dessert under a preheated broiler about 2″ from the heat for 30 seconds or until the marshmallows are golden. Let dessert cool completely and cut into squares.

Nestle Company named the Baby Ruth candy bar in honor of Grover Cleveland's first child, Ruth.

Sour Cream Raisin Bars

Makes 24 bars

Crust:

1 C. butter, softened
1¾ C. rolled oats
1¾ C. flour
1 C. brown sugar
1 tsp. baking soda

Raisin mixture:

2 C. raisins
Dash salt
2 eggs
1½ C. sugar
3 T. cornstarch
2 C. sour cream

Preheat oven to 350°. In a medium bowl, mix butter, rolled oats, flour, brown sugar and baking soda until crumbly. Set aside 1½ cups of mixture for topping. Press remaining mixture into a slightly greased and floured 9 x 13″ pan. Bake for 15 minutes. Meanwhile in a medium saucepan, boil ½ cup water, raisins and salt together for 5 minutes. Set aside. In a separate saucepan, mix eggs, sugar, cornstarch and sour cream. Boil and stir until thick and well-blended. Add raisin mixture, mix well and spread over baked crust. Crumble the reserved crust mixture over the top. Bake for an additional 20 minutes. Cool and cut into bars.

Raspberry Cheesecake Bars

Makes 32 bars

1¼ C. flour
½ C. brown sugar
½ C. finely chopped sliced almonds
½ C. butter, softened
2 (8 oz.) pkgs. cream cheese, softened
⅔ C. sugar
2 eggs
¾ tsp. almond extract
1 C. seedless raspberry preserves
½ C. flaked coconut
½ C. sliced almonds

Preheat oven to 350°. In a medium bowl, combine flour, brown sugar and chopped almonds. Cut in butter until mixture resembles fine crumbs. Set aside ½ cup of crumb mixture for topping. For crust, press remaining crumb mixture into the bottom of a greased 9 x 13″ pan. Bake for 15 minutes.

In another mixing bowl, beat the cream cheese, sugar, eggs and almond extract until smooth. Spread over the hot crust. Return to oven and bake for 15 minutes. Warm up the raspberry preserves for 15 to 30 seconds in a microwave oven. Spread preserves over cream cheese mixture. In a small bowl, combine the reserved crumb mixture, coconut and sliced almonds. Sprinkle mixture over preserves. Return to oven and bake an additional 15 minutes. Cool in the pan on a wire rack. Chill for 3 hours before cutting into bars. Store bars in refrigerator.

Rhubarb Crunch

Makes 9 servings

Bottom Crust:

½ C. flour
⅓ C. brown sugar
½ tsp. salt
½ C. unsalted butter, softened

Topping:

¾ to 1 C. sugar
½ C. flour
¾ tsp. baking powder
¼ tsp. cardamom
2 eggs
2 ½ C. chopped rhubarb

Preheat oven to 350°. In a small mixing bowl, combine flour, brown sugar and salt. Add the butter and cut it in until crumbly. Pat mixture into an 8 x 8″ square or round pan.

For the topping, in a medium bowl, combine sugar, flour, baking powder and cardamom. Set aside. In a separate bowl, beat the eggs until they are light and foamy. Whisk the mixed dry ingredients into the beaten eggs. Stir in the chopped rhubarb with a spoon and pour mixture over the crust. Bake for 40 to 45 minutes. Serve warm, with vanilla ice cream or whipped topping, if desired.

Fresh Apple Cake

Makes 15 to 16 servings

Cake:

¾ C. shortening or butter, softened
1½ C. brown sugar
2 eggs
2¼ C. sifted flour
¾ tsp. ground cinnamon
¾ tsp. ground nutmeg
1½ tsp. soda
½ tsp. salt
3 C. finely chopped apples

Topping:

¾ C. brown sugar
2 T. butter, softened
½ C. chopped walnuts

Preheat oven to 350°. In a medium bowl with an electric mixer, cream together shortening and 1½ cups of brown sugar. Add eggs and mix well. In separate bowl, stir together flour, cinnamon, nutmeg, soda and salt. Add dry mixture to creamed mixture and mix well. Stir in chopped apples. Spread mixture in a greased 9 x 13″ pan.

Prepare topping in a small bowl by blending together ¾ cup brown sugar, 2 tablespoons butter and chopped walnuts. Crumble topping mixture over the cake in the pan. Bake for 35 minutes. This cake is delicious plain or served with vanilla ice cream or whipped cream.

Carrot Cake with Cream Cheese Frosting

Makes 18 servings

2 C. sugar
2 C. flour
1½ C. vegetable oil
4 eggs
2 tsp. ground cinnamon
2 tsp. baking soda
1 tsp. salt
4 C. shredded carrots

Frosting:

1 (8 oz.) pkg. cream cheese, softened
½ C. butter or margarine, softened
2 tsp. vanilla extract
4 C. powdered sugar

Preheat oven to 350°. In large bowl with electric mixer, beat together the sugar, flour, vegetable oil, eggs, cinnamon, baking soda and salt. Stir in the shredded carrots. Pour batter into a greased 9 x 13″cake pan. Bake for 35 minutes or until a toothpick inserted in the center comes out clean. Let cake cool. Use a medium bowl and electric mixer to prepare frosting. Beat together the cream cheese, butter and vanilla. Gradually beat in the powdered sugar and beat until smooth. If frosting is too thick to spread, add small amounts of milk to reach desired consistency. Spread frosting over cooled cake.

Simple Flag Cake

Makes 12 servings

1 recipe of your favorite white or yellow cake (a mix or from scratch)

2 pts. fresh strawberries

1⅓ C. fresh blueberries

1 (12 oz.) carton whipped topping

Following recipe or package directions, prepare and bake your favorite cake in a 9 x 13″ pan. Let it cool completely. Slice 1 cup of strawberries. Cut remaining strawberries into halves. Cover cake in pan with sliced strawberries and 1 cup of the blueberries. Cover cake and berries with all of whipped topping. Arrange remaining strawberry halves and blueberries on the whipped topping to create a 'stars and stripes' flag design. Refrigerate until ready to serve.

Red Velvet Cake

Makes 3 round cakes or a 9 x 13″ cake

Cake:

½ C. shortening
1½ C. sugar
2 eggs
1 to 2 (1 oz.) bottles red food coloring
1 tsp. vanilla extract
2½ C. sifted cake flour
½ tsp. salt
2 tsp. unsweetened cocoa powder
1 C. buttermilk
1 T. white vinegar
1 tsp. baking soda

Cream Cheese Frosting:

2 (3 oz.) pkgs. cream cheese, softened
½ C. butter, softened
2 tsp. vanilla extract
4½ to 4¾ C. powdered sugar
Chopped pecans, optional

Preheat oven to 350°. In a large bowl with an electric mixer, beat shortening until fluffy. Gradually add sugar, beating well. Add eggs 1 at a time, mixing thoroughly. Stir in food coloring and vanilla. In another bowl, combine flour, salt and cocoa. Set aside. In a small bowl, combine buttermilk, vinegar and soda. Mixture will bubble. Beginning and ending with the flour mixture, alternately add flour mixture and buttermilk mixture to the shortening mixture and beat at low speed after each addition. When all ingredients are blended, beat at medium speed for 2 minutes. Pour batter into 3 greased and floured 8″ round cake pans. Bake for 25 minutes. Cool cake in pans on wire racks for 10 minutes. Remove from pans and cool completely on wire racks.

Spread cream cheese frosting between layers and on top of cake. Garnish with chopped pecans if desired.

This cake may also be prepared in a greased and floured 9 x 13″ pan. Bake for 30 minutes and cool completely on a wire rack. Spread frosting on top of cake and garnish as desired.

Quick and Easy Trifle

Makes 10 to 12 servings

- 1 cake mix, flavor of your choice
- 2 pkgs. custard or pudding mix
- 2 lbs. frozen or fresh sliced fruit
- ⅓ C. granulated sugar
- ⅓ C. fruit juice or water
- 1½ C. whipped topping
- Additional fresh fruit for garnish

Prepare cake according to package directions. Let cake cool completely. Prepare custard or pudding mix according to package instructions. Let mixture cool completely. In a large bowl, mix fruit, sugar and juice or water. Cut the cake into large chunks. Use ½ or ⅓ of each ingredient to make 2 or 3 layers in a deep glass dessert bowl. Place 1 portion of the cake chunks over the bottom of the bowl. Top with a layer of prepared fruit, then a layer of prepared custard, using equal portions of each. Repeat the process with 1 or 2 more layers of ingredients until the bowl is full. Spread top with whipped topping and garnish with pieces of fresh fruit. Scoop out servings with a large spoon.

Use any combination of cakes, puddings and fruits. Some suggestions are: angel food cake with custard and strawberries; chocolate cake with custard and cherry pie filling; chocolate cake with vanilla pudding and raspberries; angel food cake with vanilla pudding and peaches; angel food cake with custard and a combination of strawberries, raspberries and blueberries; and lemon cake with lemon pie filling and raspberries.

Good and Fast Hot Fudge Sauce

Makes 1½ cups

1 (5 oz.) chocolate bar (dark chocolate makes good blend)

1 (14 oz.) can sweetened condensed milk

Melt the chocolate bar in the microwave for 1 minute. Remove and stir. Add the sweetened condensed milk and return to microwave for 1 minute. Remove and stir again. Serve immediately or store in refrigerator until needed. Sauce is delicious over ice cream, fruit or pound cake.

Fruit Pizza

Makes 16 to 20 servings

1 (20 oz.) pkg. refrigerated sugar cookie dough
1 (8 oz.) pkg. cream cheese, softened
¼ C. powdered sugar
1 (8 oz.) carton frozen whipped topping
2 to 3 kiwifruit, peeled and thinly sliced
1 to 2 firm bananas, peeled and sliced
1 (11 oz.) can mandarin oranges, drained
½ C. red grape halves
¼ C. sugar
¼ C. orange juice
1 T. lemon juice
1½ tsp. cornstarch
Pinch salt

Preheat oven to 375°. Slice cookie dough into pieces and press dough into ungreased 14″ pizza pan. Bake crust for 10 to 12 minutes or until lightly browned. Cool completely. In a medium mixing bowl, beat the cream cheese and powdered sugar until smooth. Fold in whipped topping. Spread over the baked and cooled crust. Arrange fruit on top in a circular pattern.

In a small saucepan, bring sugar, orange juice, 2 tablespoons water, lemon juice, cornstarch and salt to a boil, stirring constantly. Boil for 2 minutes or until thickened. Cool mixture. Brush over fruit. Chill. Cut into slices. Store in refrigerator.

No-Sugar Apple Pie

Makes 6 to 8 servings

3 T. cornstarch
1 T. ground cinnamon
½ tsp. nutmeg
1 (12 oz.) can unsweetened apple juice concentrate, thawed, divided
6 C. peeled and sliced sweet, crisp apples
2 (9″) refrigerated flat pastry crusts, unbaked

Preheat oven to 350°. In a small bowl, whisk together the cornstarch, cinnamon, nutmeg and ⅓ cup apple juice concentrate. Set aside. In a large saucepan, simmer sliced apples with remaining apple juice concentrate for about 10 minutes or until tender. Stir in cornstarch mixture and continue to simmer until thickened. Remove from heat. Press 1 pastry crust into a pie pan. Spoon the apple mixture into the crust. Cover with top crust. Seal and flute the edges. Cut steam vents in top crust. Bake for 45 minutes or until crust is golden brown.

Sour Cream Peach Pie

Makes 6 servings

½ C. brown sugar
1 T. cornstarch
½ tsp. ground cinnamon
¼ tsp. ground nutmeg
Dash salt
5 C. sliced fresh peaches
1 (9″) baked pie shell
1½ C. sour cream

Preheat oven to 400°. In a large bowl, combine brown sugar, cornstarch, cinnamon, nutmeg and salt. Add peach slices and toss until coated. Spoon peach mixture into the baked pie crust. Stir sour cream and spread it over the fruit. Cover crust edges with foil. Bake for 25 minutes or until crust is golden. Serve hot or cold.

James Madison and his wife, Dolley, introduced a new dessert to the White House – ice cream. It was vanilla served with no toppings.

Popular Pumpkin Pie

Makes 6 to 8 servings

Crust:

1½ C. flour

¼ C. cold butter, cubed

¼ C. cold shortening, cubed

1½ tsp. sugar

Filling:

3 eggs, lightly beaten

2 C. canned pumpkin

1¾ C. whipping cream

¾ C. dark brown sugar

¼ C. sugar

2 T. flour

1 T. molasses

1½ tsp. ground cinnamon

1 tsp. ground ginger

¼ tsp. ground nutmeg

¼ tsp. ground cloves

¼ tsp. salt

Preheat oven to 375°. In a medium bowl, combine flour, butter, shortening and sugar. Blend together with hands until mixture resembles small crumbs. Add 5 tablespoons water and toss until well-mixed. Form the dough into a ball and knead for 30 seconds. Dust dough with flour, wrap in plastic wrap and refrigerate for at least 1 hour. Roll out dough into an 11″ circle. Place in a 9″ pie plate. Trim off all but 1″ of excess dough from sides of pie plate. Fold remaining excess dough under crust and pinch to seal. Prick bottom of pie shell with a fork and refrigerate 1 hour. Weigh crust down with beans or pie weights and bake for 10 minutes. Remove beans or weights and bake an additional 5 minutes.

In large bowl, gently beat together all filling ingredients. Pour into the baked crust. Cover crust edges with foil. Bake for 40 minutes or until filling is set.

Old-Fashioned Banana Cream Pie

Makes 6 servings

3 T. cornstarch
1 (14 oz.) can sweetened condensed milk
3 egg yolks, beaten
2 T. butter
1 tsp. vanilla extract
3 medium bananas, divided
1 (9″) pie crust, baked
1 T. lemon juice
Whipped cream

In a heavy saucepan, dissolve cornstarch in 1⅔ cups of water. Stir in the sweetened condensed milk and egg yolks. Cook and stir over medium-low heat until thickened and bubbly. Remove from heat and add butter and vanilla. Cool slightly. Slice 2 bananas. Dip banana slices in lemon juice and drain. Arrange bananas on bottom of prepared crust. Pour filling over bananas. Cover with plastic wrap and chill for 4 hours or until set.

Spread whipped cream on top of pie. Slice remaining banana, dip slices in lemon juice and drain. Garnish top of pie with banana slices. Refrigerate leftovers.

Heavenly Lemon Meringue Pie

Makes 8 servings

1 (9″) baked pie shell
5 eggs, separated
3 to 4 lemons
1½ C. sugar, divided
⅓ C. cornstarch
3 T. butter
⅛ tsp. cream of tartar
Pinch salt

Set aside the baked and cooled pie crust. Separate the egg yolks from the whites, placing the whites aside in a grease-free, straight-sided glass bowl. Set the yolks aside in a small bowl. Grate 2 teaspoons of zest from the lemons and set aside. Squeeze lemons to get ½ cup juice including pulp, but no seeds.

In a medium saucepan, combine 1 cup sugar with cornstarch. Add 1½ cups of water slowly, stirring until smooth. Add the egg yolks and stir until smooth. Place the saucepan over medium-low heat and bring contents to a slow boil, stirring constantly. Boil for 1 minute. Remove from heat and stir in the lemon juice, lemon zest and butter. Set filling aside to cool.

Preheat oven to 400°. To make meringue, add the cream of tartar and salt to the egg whites. Beat with an electric mixer at medium speed until foamy. Gradually add ½ cup sugar and continue beating on high speed until stiff peaks form.

Spoon the cooled lemon filling into the prepared pie shell, smoothing the top. With a large, clean spoon, spread a ½″ flat layer of meringue over the filling and onto the inner edge of the crust to seal it. Then spoon the remaining meringue on top of pie, shaping it into high peaks. Bake pie in the center of the oven for 6 to 8 minutes or until the meringue is golden and tips are flecked with brown. Cool pie on a wire rack.

Kentucky Chocolate Bourbon Pie

Makes 8 servings

2 eggs, beaten
½ C. butter, melted
4 tsp. bourbon
¼ C. cornstarch
¼ C. corn syrup
1 C. sugar
1 C. chopped pecans
1 (12 oz.) bag semi-sweet chocolate chips
1 (9″) unbaked pie shell
Whipped cream, optional

Preheat oven to 350°. In medium bowl, combine eggs, melted butter, bourbon, cornstarch, corn syrup and sugar. Mix well. Stir in pecans and chocolate chips. Pour mixture into unbaked pie shell. Bake for 45 to 50 minutes. Serve warm, topped with whipped cream.

Once the dinner bell rang, President Washington had a rule that all guests must be seated within five minutes.

Index

Anchors Away for Appetizers & Snacks

Salute to Soups & Sandwiches

Star Spangled Salads & Sides

Hats Off to Hot Dishes

Drum Roll for Desserts